Endorsements

Biblical scholar Christian Eberhart unpacks the words of institution of Christian communion services by explaining how first-century Christians would have understood "This is my body, this is my blood." Using a conversational style, Professor Eberhart makes his extensive scholarship accessible to a non-academic audience. Readers will find their own experience of communion deepened after reading this book.

—Rev. Dr. Priscilla Eppinger,
Professor of Religion
Community of Christ Seminary at Graceland University

With a wink and a nod to Dinah Washington and her 1959 Grammy Award winning song "What a Difference a Day Makes," Dr. Eberhart has produced an accessible explanation of the sacrament of Communion. The book is engaging, relevant, and a concise tool that helps the average churchgoer understand this essential Christian practice. Dr. Eberhart is skilled at linking key Scripture passages that unpack past traditions and illuminate today's practices at the Lord's Table. Readers will be equipped with a vocabulary that enables them to explore their own Christian faith in a deeper way and engage in dialogue with others of differing faith traditions to share the beauty of this important sacrament. I serve as a campus minister at the University of Houston and can't wait to introduce students to this refreshing discussion.

—Rev. Laureen Suba
Executive Director
United Campus Ministry of Greater Houston

No rite is more central and no practice is more formative to Christian communities than Holy Communion, also called the Eucharist or the Lord's Supper. Professor Christian Eberhart takes his readers on an enlightening journey through Scripture and history to show how these ancient texts can still speak to modern audiences. Laity and clergy alike will benefit greatly from his thought-provoking study. Well written. Insightful. Highly recommended.

—Dr. David B. Capes
Academic Dean and Professor of New Testament
Houston Graduate School of Theology

WHAT A DIFFERENCE A MEAL MAKES

THE LAST SUPPER IN THE BIBLE AND IN THE CHRISTIAN CHURCH

DR. CHRISTIAN A. EBERHART

TRANSLATED BY MICHAEL PUTMAN

LUCIDBOOKS

What a Difference a Meal Makes: The Last Supper in the Bible and in the Christian Church
Copyright © 2016 by Christian A. Eberhart

Published by Lucid Books in Houston, TX.
www.LucidBooks.net

First Printing 2016

ISBN 10: 1-63296-082-6
ISBN 13: 978-1-63296-082-5
eISBN 10: 1-63296-083-4
eISBN 13: 978-1-63296-083-2

Photo credit: Pages 132, 133, 134, 135: Christian Eberhart
Illustration credit: Page 45: Yanis Eberhart

Cover art by Dr. He Qi (www.heqiart.com), used with permission from the artist.

Special Sales: Most Lucid Books titles are available in special quantity discounts. Custom imprinting or excerpting can also be done to fit special needs. Contact Lucid Books at info@lucidbooks.net.

For Josianne
the nurse in Marseille, France,
who hosted five strangers and provided meals for them
on January 7 and 8, 2009 in the midst of a snowstorm
that was as surprising as it was powerful.

Table of Contents

Table of Contents

Acknowledgements

This book is the result of a number of workshops, seminars, and conferences that I have taught and led in various churches and at synod conventions on topics such as the Last Supper, the life and death of Jesus, and sacrifice and atonement. At such events, I was repeatedly asked to offer some of the complex concepts in a concise form. This book is my attempt to honor these requests.

I would like to express my gratitude to those who invited me to speak at such venues, and to all who attended them. These opportunities and the many questions they sparked in conversation have always motivated me to further reflect on the subject matter.

I also wish to thank my scholarly colleagues, particularly at the Annual Conference of the Society of Biblical Literature (Atlanta, GA), whose profound knowledge and stimulating presentations inspired me and helped me develop my own thoughts. I have written other books on broader subject matter, which are dedicated to an ongoing exchange with these colleagues. Some of these works also touch upon the Communion and its Old Testament roots.[1]

While writing this book, I invited many people to discussions about the topic of Communion. Some of them penned their own personal understanding of this important Christian celebration. These people belong to a variety of Christian denominations and churches—and even to different countries. Some of them attend worship regularly, while some do not, and most are laypeople. I have integrated many of their statements and testimonies. Unfortunately, there was not enough space for each one, but they all show the opinions of different people on the subject of Communion. Sometimes these opinions are similar, sometimes they are very different, but they are always truly creative and original. These quotations demonstrate to me that individuals deeply engage their own reason and have many important questions. To these people I express my deep gratefulness for their thoughts and insights. Since these personal statements and testimonies are so interesting, I decided to insert some of them here (other statements appear at the beginning of later chapters of this book):

> The Lord's Supper is a community meal, both "real" and "symbolic" that symbolizes the Christian community coming together and partaking in the body of Christ.
> *—Anonymous*

> Communion is tasting, seeing, smelling "of faith," that is to say, God can be perceived in other ways than hearing and reading. Thus, forgiveness given freely by God is received by me and becomes tangible.
> *—Gudrun Behrens (41 years of age)*

> Because of my own upbringing and experience, the Eucharist is something sad and dark.
> *—Anonymous*

Sometimes my long-winded explanations of the Last Supper are interspersed by creative, succinct, and meaningful poetry by Lothar Zenetti, a Roman Catholic priest. Poets like Zenetti are rare in Christian churches today. All the more, I herewith admit my admiration of the poetical talents of one of my own relatives. It should be noted that the poems appearing in this book are translations of Zenetti's German originals.

Acknowledgements

I am specifically grateful to the Christian Faith and Life Initiative of the Louisville Institutes (Louisville, KY) that generously supported the writing of this book (and of the German and French versions) through a substantial grant. I would also like to express warm feelings of thankfulness to Mark and Becky Lanier, founders of the Lanier Theological Library (Houston, TX), and to its director Charles Mickey. They generously invited me as a "scholar in residence" at this institution while I was putting the final touches on the manuscript and hosted me during this time. The resources at their library allowed me to improve this book, and the serene setting helped me to focus on the task. I would also like to say thanks to the Lanier Theological Library staff for their friendly and caring support.

Furthermore, I appreciate Michael Putman who provided the original translation from German. (My wife Véronique and I took it upon ourselves to translate the poems of Lothar Zenetti.) I also wish to thank my colleague Rev. Dr. Priscilla Eppinger, Professor of Religion at Community of Christ Seminary, Graceland University, and Matt Johnson, who both provided many useful comments and helped with the onerous task of proofreading. Special thanks go to Casey Cease, CEO of Lucid Books, for his interest in the manuscript, and to Sammantha Lengl and Laurie Waller for the efficient and pleasant cooperation during the final work stages.

Finally, I offer my heartfelt gratitude to my wife Véronique who read the manuscript very carefully, made many valuable comments and corrections, and translated the entire text into French (available under the title: *Invités au banquet du Seigneur: La communion dans la Bible et dans l'Église chrétienne*).

Houston, TX, December 2015
C.A.E.

Introduction

THE LAST SUPPER IN THE BIBLE AND IN THE CHRISTIAN CHURCH

Many people who attend or participate in Christian worship know the celebration with bread and wine. It is known by several different names, for example, the Last Supper, the Lord's Supper, Communion, and Eucharist. But why are there different terms for the same celebration, and what do these terms mean? What actually is Communion—a ritual, a celebration, a meal, or something else? What is its origin, and what is the significance of the gestures with bread and wine? All of these various questions aim at the actual meaning, or rather meanings, of Communion. To respond to these questions, I propose to study the core texts of the Bible in regard to Communion. Eventually I shall also explore how the celebration of Communion that we know today relates to the Bible.

As we study these texts, specific text-related questions will arise: Why did Paul warn the congregation in Corinth not to participate in Communion "unworthily"? Is this still relevant today? Does Communion center on the death of Jesus or his sacrifice? What actually is the "blood of the covenant" that is mentioned during Communion? What is the Passover? How is it possible that a ritual with bread and wine can have the power to eliminate human sins? And, to ask more generally, how can bread and wine possibly affect something that is relevant for Christians today?

All of these questions and concerns are interesting and important. Some of us may want to know more about Communion in order to participate in its practice in a more meaningful way. Or perhaps some of us have problems with certain ideas about Communion. Some of us are curious about how Communion was celebrated in the past, and how other Christian denominations understand Communion today. In short, if you are a curious person who wants to know more about what is common among most Christians, then I invite you to read this book!

The following chapters also include specific historical information that highlights the life and times of Jesus, so we are better able to understand his culture. This information is provided in additional boxes throughout each chapter and appears with the title "History and Background." Likewise, occasional footnotes contain further arguments and facts on particular details that may be of interest for those who want to learn more.

This book doesn't exhaustively explore all aspects of the topic of Communion. It certainly does not deal with or summarize all pertinent opinions, discussions, church statements, or doctrines. It is intended, rather, for laypeople in the church to gain a solid biblical foundation of the Last Supper or Communion. This book is, in fact, the result of several seminars and conferences I have taught and led in various churches and at synod conventions on topics such as the Last Supper, the life and death of Jesus, and sacrifice and atonement. After speaking at many of these sorts of events, I was repeatedly asked to offer some of the complex concepts in a concise form. This book is my attempt to honor these requests.

In the following chapters, I shall closely explore foundational texts in the Bible to determine the meaning(s) of the Last Supper or Communion. According to Mark 14:22–25, the oldest Gospel passage on this celebration, Jesus had a Passover meal with his disciples on the day before his death. At that occasion, he instituted a short, ritualized meal with bread and wine, commonly called the "Last Supper." His words of institution suggest that the sharing of the bread and wine had special significance. According to Matthew, the cup of wine contains the "blood of the covenant, which is poured out for many for the forgiveness of sins" (26:28), prompting the question of how forgiveness can be affected through wine. Luke writes about two cups of wine during the Last Supper (22:17, 20) and relates an additional story in which the disciples recognize the resurrected Jesus during the breaking of the bread (24:13–35), hinting at its highly symbolic significance for the entire mission of Jesus. The Gospel according to John omits the Last Supper proper; in its place, Jesus washes the feet of his disciples as an example of service and humility. Particularly concerned about unity in Christian congregations, the Apostle Paul adds that those who exclude socially disadvantaged people bring "judgment upon themselves" during the Communion.

These New Testament texts on the Last Supper of Jesus or the Communion prompt further studies of specific Old Testament topics, namely Passover, atonement, and sacrificial rituals. An important Jewish family feast, Passover was all about commemoration. Jews traditionally commemorated their salvation from slavery in Egypt; this framework contributed the element of remembrance of the life and death of Jesus to the celebration of Communion. When Jesus calls the cup of wine the "(new) covenant in my blood," he refers to a central text from the Torah, namely the covenant which God sealed with Israel at Mt. Sinai (Exod. 24). In this covenant, the "blood of the covenant" of sacrificial animals had the power to eliminate sins and make the Israelites holy. The wine at the Last Supper of Jesus has a similar function; it has the power to eliminate the sins of the disciples, thus establishing a "new covenant" with Jesus. The effect of this rite is, in the end, atonement, which is partially based on the Old Testament conception that the blood of sacrificial animals can eliminate sins upon physical contact. The Bible describes this process as purification. As the blood of Jesus, the wine of the Last Supper also purges human sins and purifies humans. It should be noted, however, that the New Testament passion narratives or the accounts of the Last Supper do not describe the death of Jesus as a ritual sacrifice.

The breaking of the bread, on the other hand, refers to New Testament texts about various meals that convey central concerns of the mission of Jesus. In antiquity, meals were events for initiating and maintaining social contacts. Such meals show that Jesus was seeking the company of people who were considered sinners and socially ostracized. Jesus had a preferential option for them. In the breaking and eating of the bread, his concern for such people was allegorized and became visible. The Last Supper is, therefore, a ritualized meal that sends a signal against the perennial tendency of humans to exclude others. Communion thereby signifies that the Kingdom of God is fundamentally open to all people.

A final chapter explores selected aspects of the practice of Communion in modern Christian churches. It makes recommendations intended for all who want to know how certain current church practices relate to foundational biblical texts. It also helps all who have an interest in aligning their own customs of celebrating Communion with those of early Christianity.

Chapter 1

DIVISION AND UNITY IN THE CHRISTIAN CHURCH

"Why don't all Christians worship together?"
"Why aren't the many Christian churches,
denominations, and groups united?" I hear
both of these questions all the time, and both are concerned with
a generally recognized problem. According to one estimate,
there are about 20,000 different Christian denominations
and church groups on the earth. When considering this

problem, we may console ourselves with a glance at other world religions. Judaism, Hinduism, Buddhism, or Islam are in no way unified religious movements either. Each of them likewise consists of hundreds, or perhaps even thousands, of different groups and sub-groups when considered globally. Christianity is not altogether in any worse condition than other religions.

Commonalities of Christian Groups and Denominations

But there is another answer to the question of the lack of unity among Christian denominations. One could also say: "We are indeed all one. We do belong together. And we do celebrate all our worship services in somewhat similar forms." But how could we arrive at this conclusion? The question regarding denominations and their worship practices could itself be questioned. Why do we say that the different Christian churches are separated? This lamentation is almost always based on the viewpoint that many Christian groups have differing beliefs and doctrines. Of course Roman Catholics, Reformed Protestants, United Protestants, Lutheran Protestants, Pentecostals, or Orthodox have different titles. On the other hand, Catholics, Protestants, and Orthodox all refer to themselves simply as "Christian." They are all named after Jesus Christ. This unifies them beyond all further denominational designations. While it is true that these groups have somewhat different faith statements, most are derived from the Apostles' and Nicene Creeds. They all believe in the triune God, and these creeds are regularly recited during worship in many Christian churches. There is much unity among Christians—not just division.

Moreover, in spite of the apparent lack of unity, all Christians *worship God*. And Christians celebrate *Communion*—at least most of them. To my knowledge, there are few Christian groups that do not. For many of them, Communion is even the absolute *center* of worship and is considered a sacrament—a sacred rite in which the connection between God and humans is manifest. The Last Supper of Jesus is also one of the most commonly painted motifs in the history of art—more than four thousand different renderings of it exist. A beautiful, large painting by the Chinese artist Dr. He Qi adorns the worship space of the church my family and I attend here in Houston. Placed right behind the altar, it depicts Jesus celebrating communion with two of his followers at Emmaus. The choice of a piece of art featuring this motif shows how important the celebration of communion is for people in the congregation. I selected it also as the cover image of this book.

Christians of various denominations may certainly use different labels for this celebration. For some it is the Eucharist, for others it is the Mass or the Lord's Supper or the Last Supper or the Communion (these last two terms are the ones I shall use in this book). May I ask you how this rite is called in your church? What other labels for this rite are you familiar with?

Communion as the Common Worship Practice of Christians

Almost all Christians celebrate Communion. This is significant. It means that Christians share and eat bread and drink wine in similar ways. Naturally, there are differences. In one church, bread is literally broken, while in another, flat wafers are handed out. In some churches, only wine is drunk, while others also offer grape juice. In some churches, worshippers drink from a common cup while in others, small cups are distributed. Some churches don't share these customs at all but instead dip the bread into the cup. In certain Roman Catholic churches, only the priest and a few others drink the wine, whereas the lay worshippers receive only the host or a piece of bread.

Aside from these differences, some Christians celebrate Communion more frequently than others. For many Christians, Communion is a regular part of their Sunday worship services; others celebrate it less often, for example once per month or perhaps only four times a year. Jehovah's Witnesses usually celebrate Communion just once a year. Yet there are those churches that celebrate it daily. The list of such differences could be extended. In reality, there is no uniform Christian practice of Communion. But to say it once more: almost all Christians celebrate this meal of bread and wine in one form or another. One could add that the celebration of Communion connects contemporary Christians with the early church, and with all Christians throughout history, in so far as almost all of them have celebrated Communion.

These observations are a comfort to many Christians. But there's also another consideration: we all have slightly different understandings of the meaning behind eating the broken bread and drinking the wine (or grape juice). Different denominations have disagreed over the correct understanding of Communion for years. As already stated, Communion goes by many terms. And Communion is celebrated in different forms.

We can't deny that these differences in fact exist—and it is one of the purposes of this book to show those differences, which we will discover together. Later I will delve into a few of these differences—though of course not all of them. But for now, I would like to emphasize that in spite of the lack of uniformity in doctrine, worship, and practice, the Christian ritual of eating bread and drinking wine *does unite Christians*.

On the pages that follow, you will certainly find concepts

and customs of celebrating Communion that are familiar to you. I hope that you will learn something about their origin and meaning. On the other hand, you will surely encounter ideas, interpretations, and forms of celebrating Communion that are unfamiliar, or which you don't approve of. Even so, I hope you'll remain open and curious about other faith traditions and the historical practices of early Christians. Thus you can learn new things about an old, but important, celebration. In this way, I invite you to discover the amazing power that Communion has in today's broken world. I invite you to see for yourself what a difference a meal makes.

Chapter 2

COMMUNION IN THE NEW TESTAMENT

Most Christians agree that Communion is important. In many churches, it is one of the central events of the service. So why do Christians celebrate Communion in their worship?

The origins of the celebration of Communion are found in the Christian Bible. We read in the New Testament that Jesus Christ hosted a last supper with his disciples before he was crucified. According to three of the four Gospels, Jesus offered bread and wine to his disciples during this meal (Matt. 26:26–29; Mark 14:22–25; Luke 22:15–20). Thus, whenever Christians celebrate Communion they are to some degree imitating what

Jesus once did. In addition, the Apostle Paul, in one of his letters to the Corinthians, makes suggestions as to how Communion is to be celebrated (1 Cor. 11:23–25). Brief comments in this text and others in the New Testament make clear that the first Christians were already celebrating Communion regularly. Later Christian texts permit us to see how this practice gradually developed. So what can we know about these New Testament texts? How do they depict the communion practice in the early Christian church? Is this practice always the same or are there differences?

In this book, we shall be concerned with reading and understanding the texts of the Bible, and we shall study them carefully, one by one. In my opinion, we respect a text when we read it thoroughly and reflect upon its meaning. This process may yield wide-ranging insights, and prompt many questions which we shall get to in due time. First, we shall consider some texts in the Gospel of Mark.

The Last Supper in the Gospel according to Mark

Today, most biblical scholars suppose that the Gospel according to Mark is the oldest of the four New Testament Gospels and was produced around 70 CE. This Gospel in itself was most likely composed from accounts about Jesus dating from some decades prior to its writing. Therefore we shall study this text first.

The Gospel according to Mark tells of the actions of Jesus, and of his death and the empty tomb.[2] One of the last things that Jesus did before his crucifixion was to ask his disciples to prepare a supper which he wanted to share with them (Mark 14:12–16). This was to be a Passover meal since the passion of Jesus happened during the time of the Passover feast and the Festival of Unleavened Bread. The Passover was an ancient Jewish festival involving hearty eating and drinking.[3] With this in mind, we read in the Gospel according to Mark:

> And when they [Jesus and his disciples] were eating, he took bread and after blessing it broke it and gave it to them and said, "Take; this is my body." And he took a cup and gave it to them after giving thanks, and they all drank from it. And he said to them, "This is my blood of the covenant, which is poured out for many. Truly I tell you that I will not again drink of the fruit of the vine until that day when I drink it anew in the kingdom of God." (14:22–25)[4]

This text may be more or less familiar to those among you who have participated in Communion services. But perhaps you notice that it differs in several instances from the words spoken by your pastor or priest during the Eucharistic service. The reason for this is that the different New Testament accounts of the Last Supper present differences in wording. For the worship of our Christian churches, these different versions were all merged into a variety of unified, composite forms within our denominations. These forms, however, are not exactly identical with any one account of the Last Supper in the New Testament.

In the Last Supper account in Mark, Jesus gave his disciples bread and a cup of wine. Jesus spoke over the bread and the cup to institute this celebration. In the church today, these words of Jesus are called the "words of institution." They are the reason that the first disciples and Christians all over the world since have concluded that bread and cup have special meaning and are about more than just eating and drinking. Conceptually, eating food in remembrance of salvation was already familiar to those who partook of the Jewish Passover. But Jesus offered his own interpretation: "Take; this is my body," he said during the distribution of the bread. That is very terse. And after his disciples had drunk the wine, Jesus said, "This is my blood of the covenant, which is poured out for many."

We may be tempted to take these words for granted as they may sound familiar. But is it really clear what they mean? Is it self-explanatory if someone were to share bread and a cup of wine and say to the recipients, "this is my body and blood"? Also note that Jesus was saying this to the disciples when he was present with them.

Why would Jesus call wine in a cup his "blood"? In early Judaism, the idea that wine could represent blood was rather common. At that time, the expression "*blood* of grapes" was used to mean the *juice* of grapes (Gen. 49:11; Deut. 32:14).[5] The word "blood" obviously substitutes for the word "juice." Wine and blood look similar since both are red liquids. But these phrases of the Old Testament do not imply that juice had changed to blood. Moreover the expression to "drink blood like wine" is also found in the Old Testament (Zech. 9:15). When Jesus said during Communion that the wine was blood, he was making use of an expression familiar to the Jews of his day. His disciples understood these words right away.

An interesting detail about that first Communion is the timing, that is, when Jesus spoke the words of institution. In Mark's text we just read, "And he [Jesus] took a cup and gave it to them after giving thanks, and they all drank from it. And he said to them, 'This is my blood of the covenant.'" (Mark 14:23–24). The order of events makes it clear that Jesus spoke the second word of institution after he had given his disciples the cup and they had drunk. Jesus offers his interpretation not prior to, but *after* the event.

Aside from that, in Mark's scene about the Last Supper, Jesus said nothing as to what the consumption of the bread was supposed to affect. He said simply, "This is my body." And what can it mean when Jesus said about the wine that his disciples had drunk: "This is my blood of the covenant"? These words are likely familiar to us since we have heard them frequently during worship. But do we know what they mean? Jesus added that this blood is "poured out for many." These words, though familiar, may sound vague, too. Do they refer to the forgiveness of sins? If so, why does the text say that *all* drank from the cup (Mark 14:23), if the blood was poured out only for *many* (14:24)? What does the difference between "all" and "many" mean?

Later we shall explore in detail what Jesus implied with his words of institution over bread and wine.[6] Here I would just like to explain that the words "the blood of the covenant" formed a fixed expression familiar to the disciples and to others of that time. Almost 2,000 years later, however, they are not widely known or understood. Even those among us who repeatedly hear about them at church do not automatically know exactly what they mean. Hence it is necessary that we familiarize ourselves with some customs of the Jewish religion of 2,000 years ago. This means we will get to know the world of Jesus a little better. Then the words of Jesus over the bread and wine will begin to make sense.

Jesus also added a few words regarding his future fate: "Truly I tell you that I will not again drink of the fruit of the vine until that day when I drink it anew in the kingdom of God" (Mark 14:25). Jesus thus indicated that he was eating his last supper. He foresaw his own death, so the atmosphere of this meal would likely have been marked by a sense of sorrow. Yet these words contain a glimpse of hope as well. He didn't expect his impending death to be the end of the story. Instead, he looked forward in anticipation to a life after death in the kingdom of God.

Moreover, the atmosphere of this meal was marked with tension. Just before supper, Jesus had announced his betrayer was dining with them (Mark 14:18), prompting a few urgent questions: *Who* was this betrayer? *How* would he carry out his betrayal? Could Jesus perhaps still *save himself*? As we already know from the Gospel stories, the betrayer was Judas, one of the twelve. The danger Jesus faced didn't only come from his enemies (Mark 3:1; 14:1–2), but from one of those who surrounded him every day and followed him. It was a threat "from within." In this regard, the situation of Jesus was different from the historical occasion that the Jews commemorated in their Passover feast, which was the delivery out of Egypt. At that time, the threat came from the Egyptians; it from "from outside" or "from the other." Thus the Last Supper was not just like a Passover feast. It was something new. It was a feast that included an "inside threat."

Mark's account of the Last Supper also states repeatedly that Jesus and the disciples ate together *while*, and perhaps *before* the Last Supper proper began. "And when they were reclining at table[7] *and eating*, Jesus said [that one of his disciples would betray him]" (Mark 14:18). This happened before the Last Supper, properly speaking. And the first sentence of the passage concerned with the actual Last Supper declares, "And *when they ate,* he [Jesus] took bread" (14:22). This means that the ritualized meal with bread and wine that Christians came to call "Last Supper" actually happened in the context of a longer and more opulent meal. Since the words Jesus spoke over the cup (14:24–25) are immediately followed by a remark that Jesus and his disciples departed to go to the Mount of Olives (14:26), the short meal rite might have marked the conclusion of the opulent meal. By the way, the biblical text does not specify what Jesus and his disciples ate during this longer meal. Roasted lamb might have been included, though, as earlier the disciples had explicitly asked where they were to prepare the Passover lamb (14:12). Jesus and the disciples likely ate this lamb later in the evening.

Another feature of Jesus' supper was that it did not occur

at the Jerusalem Temple or in any other religious location. Instead, Jesus celebrated it with his disciples in some random room in some random house (Mark 14:13–14). This implies an entirely ordinary and everyday environment. One could say that "suits" Jesus. Incidentally, the Gospels never portrayed him as being involved in any of the known sects that constituted Judaism back then. He did share with the Pharisees the belief in the resurrection of the dead, but he was himself no Pharisee. He once withdrew to the desert (Matt. 4:1–2; Mark 1:12–13), but he did not live there continuously, as was the habit of the Jewish community in Qumran.[8] He asked the man whom he had cured of a skin disease to bring the prescribed sacrifices to the temple (Mark 1:40–45). But he was no priest.

It "fits" with this picture that Jesus called disciples who were also not recognized as religious experts. The Gospels report that they had worked as fishermen on the Sea of Galilee (Mark 1:16–20) and as tax collectors (2:13–17). Because of this, the Scribes and the Pharisees, who were "official representatives" of Judaism back then, criticized Jesus. They considered some of his followers to be sinners (Matt. 9:11–13; Mark 2:16–17; Luke 5:30).[9] This means Jesus and his disciples lived conspicuously apart from the representatives and key places of the established religion of his time. Moreover, the short Last Supper ritual with bread and wine which Jesus instituted at the end of his Passover meal also "fit" such aspects: it featured no lengthy or elaborate ritual, and the New Testament texts record that it did not agree fully with any of the religious customs back then.

Conclusion: According to the oldest Gospel of the New Testament, Jesus celebrated a somewhat opulent Passover meal with his disciples on the day before his death. In the context of this feast, and perhaps toward its conclusion, he used bread and a cup of wine to institute a short, ritualized meal. The latter is what Christians came to call the "Last Supper." Jesus spoke the words of institution, words which suggest that the sharing of the bread and wine had special significance. First, the words of institution convey that the bread and wine represented the body and blood of Jesus. Second, Jesus interpreted this "blood" as his "blood of the covenant." Interestingly he added this phrase of interpretation after the disciples had drunk the cup. Finally, the celebration of the Last Supper occurred in a rather tense and sorrowful atmosphere, as the passion and death of Jesus were close at hand. At the same time, however, Jesus expressed the hope to be in the kingdom of God after his death.

The Last Supper in the Gospel according to Matthew

The Gospel according to Matthew is the first in the sequence of New Testament writings; however, it was probably written between the years 85 and 90 CE, and therefore 15 or 20 years later than the Gospel according to Mark. Much of the information about Jesus in Matthew agrees with what Mark tells us. Many biblical scholars are therefore of the opinion that Matthew's Gospel has derived a large portion of its own content more or less directly from Mark. This content was then interwoven especially with the sayings of Jesus that were recorded in yet another source. So Matthew usually gives a fuller picture of the life of Jesus.

The Gospel according to Matthew also features the story of the Last Supper of Jesus. The passage states the following:

> But when they were eating, Jesus took bread and broke it after blessing it and said as he gave it to the disciples, "Take, eat; this is my body." And he took a cup and gave it to them after giving thanks and said, "Drink from it,

all of you, for this is my blood of the covenant, which is poured out for many for the forgiveness of sins. I tell you, I will not again drink of this fruit of the vine until that day when I drink it anew with you in my Father's kingdom." (Matt. 26:26–29)

We notice that this excerpt is similar to the account of Mark, which we just examined. But the two are not completely identical. If we were to underline or highlight the discrepancies between the two narratives of the Last Supper, what stands out?

The most important differences between the two Gospels follow a certain pattern. First, after the word "take," Matthew adds the invitation to "eat" (Matt. 26:26). Second, in Matthew Jesus says, "drink from it, all of you" as he hands the cup to the disciples (26:27). In the Gospel according to Mark, the corresponding words are narrative: "and they all drank from it" (Mark 14:23). Both sentences are thus comparable in content. In Mark, however, the command to drink is not included. In Matthew, it appears in analogy to the foregoing command to "eat" (Matt. 26:26). Third, the words "drink from it, all of you" are connected to the word of institution referring to the cup. Thus, the invitation to drink the wine occurs at the same time as the interpretation. The word of institution doesn't appear after the drinking of the cup as in the Gospel according to Mark (see above, p. 16).

Fourth, the Gospel according to Matthew adds, "for the forgiveness of sins" to the words "this is my blood of the covenant, which is poured out for many" (Matt. 26:28). The Gospel according to Mark was not entirely clear as to what the drinking of wine actually accomplished, but the Gospel according to Matthew eliminates the ambiguity. However, I had observed above that, according to Mark 14:23, *all* drank from the cup, although Jesus said that his blood would be poured out for *many* according to Mark 14:24. The same observation now applies to Matthew 26:27–28. Is the "forgiveness of sins" not for all disciples? Is Judas Iscariot, one of the twelve disciples, possibly excluded from the forgiveness because he would later betray Jesus (Mark 14:44–46; Matthew 26:48–50)? This is, however, not the intention of Mark or Matthew. The choice of terminology is most likely due to an earlier statement of Jesus about himself. According to Matthew 20:28 (and also Mark 10:45), he had said that "the Son of Man did not come to be served, but to serve and give his life as a ransom for many." It is likely that Jesus referred to this key statement about his mission. Moreover, the Greek word for "many" actually means "a whole lot," which does not stand in sharp contrast to the term "all." These words, therefore, do not diminish the effectiveness of the forgiveness of sins through the Last Supper of Jesus.

Finally, Matthew also inserts a few words into the statement of Jesus that convey both his sorrow because of his impending death and his hope to be in God's kingdom. Jesus says he expects to drink wine in his Father's kingdom "with you," that is, with his disciples (Matt. 26:29). Mark's Gospel features the corresponding words in a tone of farewell, while Matthew's version is characterized by the confidence that Jesus will be reunited, and celebrate anew, with his followers.

When we review these modifications, we can observe the following tendency: Matthew supplements the text of Mark's Gospel in order to provide more clarity (he also adds the word "Jesus" in Matt. 26:26). He likewise strengthens the hortatory character of the words of Jesus by adding the appeals to "eat" and "drink."

Conclusion: By and large, the Gospel according to Matthew adopts the account of the Last Supper found in Mark. Small modifications, such as the appeals to eat the bread and drink the wine, are intended to further clarify certain actions.

Moreover, Matthew explicitly states that drinking from the cup aims at "the forgiveness of sins." Finally, the invitation to drink from the cup of wine is now connected to the respective word of institution. This means, in terms of chronological sequence, the latter could have occurred before or simultaneously with the drinking.

The Last Supper in the Gospel according to Luke

The Gospel according to Luke was probably written at the same time as the Gospel according to Matthew—i.e., about 85 or 90 CE. With the Gospel of Matthew, there is speculation that perhaps some of its content might have been taken from another shorter source. But the situation is different with respect to Luke: he explicitly tells his readers about the origins of his information (see below, p. 25).

In the Gospel according to Luke, the Last Supper is also part of the passion narrative of Jesus. Read the following scene of the Last Supper attentively. Those of you who have good recollections of the corresponding scenes according to Mark and Matthew—or who recall the order of Communion celebrations in your own churches—might be surprised.

> And he [Jesus] said to them [the disciples], "I have very much desired to eat this Passover with you before I suffer. For I tell you that I will not eat it again until it is fulfilled in the kingdom of God." And after taking a cup and giving thanks, he said, "Take this and divide it among yourselves. For I tell you that from now on I will not drink of the fruit of the vine until the kingdom of God comes." And after taking bread and giving thanks, he broke it and gave it to them, saying, "This is my body that is given for you; do this in remembrance of me." And he did the same with the cup after supper, saying,

"This cup is the new covenant in my blood, which is poured out for you." (Luke 22:15–20)

Instead of the usual pattern of *bread—cup*, Luke's Gospel features the sequence *cup—bread—cup*. The cup appears twice. In the first appearance, Jesus gives thanks, commands to "take" and distribute it, and says that this is his last meal. Yet here, the word of institution is missing. It appears later with "the cup after supper" (Luke 22:20) and is linked to the action of drinking in a way that—chronologically speaking—could have occurred before or simultaneously to the drinking, as in Matthew's Gospel. Yet it is different from the words of institution found in both Mark and Matthew. In this instance, the covenant is called a "*new* covenant."

The sequence *cup—bread—cup* may show that Luke emphasizes the Passover feast more strongly than the other Gospels. This is apparent at the start of the meal when Jesus says that he wants to eat "this Passover" (Luke 22:15) with his disciples. By this, he means the Passover lamb (22:7). Traditionally, during the Jewish Passover feast, numerous cups of wine were handed around. Moreover, the context of this old celebration explains why Luke added the comment "do this in remembrance of me" to the distribution of the bread (22:19). The remembrance or memorial of past salvation was an important element of the Jewish Passover feast.

It is with this idiosyncratic sequence that Luke's report of the Last Supper distinguishes itself from that of the other Gospels. There are, however, further differences as well, starting with the bread. In Mark 14:22, nothing was said about what the consumption of the bread was supposed to "effect." We only read, "this is my body," just as in Matthew 26:26. Luke 22:19 features for the first time the additional phrase "that is given for you." It is parallel to the phrase said over the cup in the

HISTORY AND BACKGROUND:

The Sources of the Gospel according to Luke

Right at the beginning, the author of this account of Jesus states in a candid and sober manner both that other accounts on his subject exist and that he has made use of them in his own writing. He is apparently not ashamed to mention this fact. He knows that doing so will win credibility for his own account. Therefore he begins with the words:

> Many have undertaken to draw up an account of the events that have occurred among us, just as they were handed down to us by those who were eyewitnesses from the beginning and servants of the word. Hence I too decided, after investigating everything carefully from the very first, to write an orderly account for you, most excellent Theophilus, so that you may know the truth concerning the things about which you have been instructed. (Luke 1:1–4)

Luke also honestly admits that he did not know Jesus personally. Instead he interviewed eyewitnesses, people who had met Jesus or were personally close to him. Moreover, he investigated diligently and probably read the Gospel according to Mark, just as Matthew had. Then he tells his story of Jesus. He uses numerous excerpts from Mark and interweaves them with information taken from other sources about Jesus, particularly Jesus' sayings.

very next verse: "which is poured out for you" (Luke 22:20). There's yet another difference here from the other Gospels, for in Mark 14:24 the corresponding expression is: "which is poured out for many" (and in Matthew 26:28 we find, "which is poured out for many for the forgiveness of sins"). Luke chose to use the words "for you" in his own text to render it easier to understand. Leaving no further ambiguity, these words clearly refer to all the disciples with whom Jesus celebrated his Last Supper.

The Gospel according to Luke, however, features a second occurrence of this special rite. Immediately after the women's account of the miraculous resurrection of Jesus, which the male disciples reject (Luke 24:1–12), we read about two disciples on the road to the village of Emmaus (24:13–35). They talk about the events that happened previously. At that moment, Jesus joins them, but they do not recognize him. The two men tell him about the incidents including the women's testimony that Jesus was apparently seen alive. Jesus then calls them "foolish ones" (24:25) because they did not believe the words of the prophets. The two disciples still do not recognize Jesus, but invite him to have supper with him. Luke continues, "When he was at the table with them, he took bread, blessed and broke it, and gave it to them. Then their eyes were opened, and they recognized him" (24:30–31).

It is noteworthy that Luke's Gospel features a second Last Supper scene. And the true identity of Jesus is only revealed because of the characteristic way in which he handles the bread. This would fit with what Luke wrote earlier. During the "first" Last Supper scene, Jesus said, "This is my body that is given for you; do this in remembrance of me" (Luke 22:19). Hence the two disciples would have done exactly this and remembered him during the breaking of the bread. I shall show later that this event is highly symbolic of the entire mission of Jesus. At any case, the disciples returned from Emmaus to Jerusalem to proclaim that Jesus has been resurrected. Furthermore, it is noteworthy that the two cups of wine, which are typical for Luke's "first" Last Supper scene, are not mentioned at all. This, too, might be due to what Jesus said back then, namely that he would not drink wine any more until the kingdom of God comes (Luke 22:18).

Conclusion: The version of the Last Supper in the Gospel according to Luke is striking for its unusual sequence of *cup—bread—cup*. It could be derived from the Passover feast just like the prompt "remembrance," which appears here for the first time and only in connection with the distribution of the bread. In addition, some phrases in the words of institution in Luke's Gospel have been adjusted to make the account easier to comprehend. Only Luke features the account of two disciples on the road to Emmaus. They are joined by the resurrected Jesus who celebrates a "second" Last Supper with them. The disciples only recognize Jesus during the bread rite, which emerges as a characteristic event of highly symbolic significance for the entire mission of Jesus.

The Last Supper in the First Letter of Paul to the Corinthians

If we follow the sequence of the New Testament writings, then we encounter the first information about the Last Supper in the Gospel according to Matthew (Matt. 26:26–29), followed by the Gospel according to Mark (Mark 14:22–25). I explained that the latter is the older of the two—it was written in about the year 70 CE. Matthew wrote about the year 85 or 90, and Luke did too. However, if we had begun with the oldest information in the New Testament about the Last Supper, then we would have read a few passages in the first letter of Paul to the community in Corinth.

HISTORY AND BACKGROUND:

The Early Christian Community in Corinth

The city of Corinth is located in Greece on the narrow isthmus between Attica and the Peloponnese. On either side of this isthmus, this city had a harbor (*Cenchrea* and *Lechaio*). Accordingly, Corinth developed into an important trading center and became the capital of the province of Achaia in the year 27 BCE. As with many other port cities, however, Corinth had a reputation for extravagance and immorality.

The early Christian community in Corinth was founded by the Apostle Paul in 50 or 51 CE. During that time, Paul lived there for about eighteen months (Acts 18:1–11). The city of Corinth brought together immigrants from different countries of the Mediterranean region as well as from different social strata. Conflict soon arose within the Christian community which later came to a head and led to the crisis between the Corinthians and Paul. The apostle tried to mitigate these problems in his letters to the Corinthians.

The oldest texts of the New Testament were written by the Apostle Paul. Already in the year 50, he had written his first letter to the Christian community in Thessalonica (modern day Salonika in Greece)—this is probably the oldest text in the New Testament! Then he wrote more letters to other communities, such as the First Letter to the Corinthians during a stay in Ephesus sometime between 54 and 56 CE.

Paul wrote this letter in response to news from some of the members of the community in Corinth that troubled him. "For it has become known to me through Chloe's [people], dear sisters and brothers, that there is strife among you" (1 Cor. 1:11). So Paul was eager to help his old friends. Before writing this letter, he had already written an earlier one, as he incidentally mentions in this writing (5:9). The "first" letter to the Corinthians in the New Testament is therefore really the second one. However, Paul's earlier letter has not been passed on and got lost.

What sorts of problems in the community were reported to Paul? To answer this question, we must call to mind a few aspects of the historical situation. First, it is important to know that in antiquity, people of high social standing did not need to work all the time. Their primary task was to order others about. In contrast, slaves, day laborers, and other people of low social rank had to work hard the entire day.

Second, it is possible to reconstruct a few details of what happened when Christians in Corinth gathered. I have already addressed this point to some extent: the narrative of Mark's Gospel gives several indications that Jesus and his disciples ate *before* the start of the actual rite of the Last Supper with bread and wine (see above, p. 18). The same applies to Matthew and Luke. Now Paul affirms as well that the celebration of Communion was the last part of a long and lavish meal. What one would eat at such an occasion depended on what the participants of the meal had brought, and these came from very differing social groups. Paul explicitly mentions this in his letter to the Corinthians—and indicates certain problems as well: "For when the time comes to eat, each of you goes ahead with your own supper, so one remains hungry and another gets drunk" (1 Cor. 11:21). The well-to-do members of the Christian communities could probably arrive early to the meal. What is more, they could bring more food along, and could naturally eat until they felt satiated. Slaves and day laborers, on the other hand, finished their work much later in the day. Since they were poorer, they were able to bring only a little food—and sometimes none at all. When they finally arrived at the gathering of the congregation, there was often hardly any food left over and they went hungry. Is it sufficient that, in the end, everyone had an opportunity to participate in the subsequent rite of Communion? In view of this situation Paul pointed to the Last Supper that Jesus celebrated with his disciples:

> For I received from the Lord what I also passed on to you, that the Lord Jesus on the night he was betrayed took bread, and after giving thanks he broke it and said, "This is my body that is for you. Do this in remembrance of me." In the same way, he took the cup also, after supper, saying, "This cup is the new covenant in my blood. Do this, whenever you drink it, in remembrance of me." For whenever you eat this bread and drink this cup, you proclaim the Lord's death until he comes. (1 Cor. 11:23–26).

Let us study this passage sentence-by-sentence. First, Paul explains that he received the information that he is now sharing as a tradition "from the Lord." Surely he meant that the Christian rite of Communion goes back to Jesus in person. Paul himself had learned of it through tradition. This happened either through the transmission of information, which would include teachings about the Last Supper, or while he attended worship (during which the celebration of Communion conveys such information as well)—or perhaps as a combination of both of these possibilities.

Then Paul continues, "on the night he was betrayed . . ." The three Gospels we have studied above do not feature such a sentence. Unlike the authors of these Gospels, however, Paul does not talk about the Last Supper in the context of a larger narrative about Jesus. He is rather addressing problems that were making life difficult for the Christians in Corinth. Nevertheless we notice that the Last Supper is connected with the passion of Jesus just like in the Gospels. Therefore, Paul speaks of the night of the betrayal. Then he talks about the familiar rite with the bread and cup and the words of institution. However, the Passover during which Jesus celebrated the Last Supper according to the Gospels remains unmentioned.

After the passage dealing with the Last Supper of Jesus in First Corinthians 11:23–26, Paul does not change his theme. He makes a few more pronouncements that show the theme of Communion was very delicate. He says that everybody who drinks of the cup and eats of the bread "unworthily" will be "guilty concerning the body and blood of the Lord" (1 Cor. 11:27). But that's not all! A person is supposed to have tested himself or herself, Paul says immediately afterwards. Whoever "does not discern the body of the Lord" eats and drinks "judgment" upon him- or herself (11:29). Paul has terrified many Christians with this definitive statement. What does it mean to discern the body of the Lord? Why does a lack of such discernment carry with it such threatening consequences? Is it because this bread is the body of Jesus?

We hit upon the answer not only later in this text, but also find that it is already given before the actual passage concerning Communion. Paul repeats the image of the body repeatedly in his letter to the Corinthians. He says, for example, "The bread that we break, is it not the communion of the body of Christ? Because there is one bread, we who are many are one body as we all partake of the one bread" (1 Cor. 10:16–17). And after the passage concerning Communion, he similarly says: "Now you are the body of Christ and individually members of it" (12:27).

Paul also seeks to convey the bread and cup as the presence, or more precisely the company of Jesus with humans. However it is equally important that the members of the community in Corinth understand themselves to be united and take the initiative to hold together as one. This is what Paul wished to emphasize with his talk of the body of Christ. He also has much to say about Communion itself, in particular regarding the "new covenant." Later we will examine the significance of this phrase.[10] For now, let it suffice to say that the term "covenant" indicates that people convene to enter into compacts with each other and to be connected. Thus the unity of many people is central to the concept of Communion. The bread as the body of Christ is "for *you*" according to First Corinthians 11:24. This pronoun "you" is not a singular, but a plural; it designates a group of persons. Here in Texas, we could translate "for *y'all*" to avoid the ambiguity. Communion is, therefore, not really for *individuals*—although no one should construe this statement to mean that Communion cannot be brought to old or sick people who live alone in their homes. When Paul wrote about the body of Jesus "for *you*," however, he implied that Communion was then, and is now, by its very nature shared with people who have come together in community. And this means that then as now, Communion involves the promotion of corporate well-being as opposed to individual salvation. That is the real reason why Paul referred to the Last Supper of Jesus in his reply to the Corinthians, who were then struggling with the problem of a schism in their community. Those who took part in Communion now belonged together! This special celebration was supposed to have helped the Corinthians with their internal problems.

On the other hand, any behavior that endangered the unity founded on the body of Jesus was to be avoided. Above all, this had to do with the conduct of the Corinthians at the supper. Paul then takes a definite position: "So then, my brothers and sisters, when you come together to eat, wait for one another. If you are hungry, eat at home, so that when you come together, it will not be for your condemnation" (1 Cor. 11:33–34). Behind this statement is the reality that Communion was still a part of a more extensive meal, during which many food items were available. It was a visible expression of unity and mutual care that everyone could eat at a common table until they were full—at least in theory. The "judgment" (or the "conviction") and the concern of eating "unworthily" were parts of a pattern of behavior that endangered the unity of the community and therefore the body of Jesus. Or, to say it differently: any behavior that perpetuated—or even further emphasized—social and other differences in the community was referred to as "eating unworthily."

Therefore, Paul wrote about the Last Supper of Jesus in order to help the community in Corinth overcome their inner divisions. He announced this central theme of his letter already at its opening: fellowship with Christ and the unity of everyone in Christ (1 Cor. 1:9). Internal divisions are mentioned next (1:10). Human fellowship is therefore dependent upon fellowship with God.

Finally, I would like to add a few more observations with regard to Paul's passage about the Last Supper. First, it should be noted that the apostle does not talk about the eating of bread or the drinking of wine. If in the Gospels the word of institution pertaining to the cup is sometimes mentioned as occurring after the drinking (Mark 14:23–24) and sometimes before it (in Matthew and Luke), then such detailed information is not at all manifest in this letter of Paul for the very reason that it contains no word about the actual consumption.

Second, the comment "do this in remembrance of me" (1 Cor. 11:24–25) follows each of the two words of institution over the bread and cup. Thus Paul emphasizes in a special way that all who eat the bread and drink from the cup are supposed to think of Jesus and the story of his life. This was necessary here since Paul did not place the passage of the Last

Supper in the context of a continuous narrative about Jesus. Instead, he suddenly spoke about it in the course of giving advice regarding the internal divisions in the Corinthian community. He considered it important that the participants in the Communion remembered or envisioned the story of Jesus. Without Jesus, Communion was and is no Communion! Later on, we shall explore this thought in more depth.[11]

And third, Paul modified the concluding sentence in which Jesus had connected the Last Supper with his death and simultaneously expressed his hope to subsequently be "in the kingdom of God." In the three Gospels which we have studied so far, this provision is linked to the drinking of the wine; here, however, Paul adds the following comment: "For whenever you eat this bread and drink this cup" (1 Cor. 11:26). Then he references once more the impending death as well as the life thereafter. The latter, nevertheless, does not appear as a provision of being in God's kingdom; instead, Paul states that Jesus will return.

Conclusion: The oldest text of the New Testament that mentions the Last Supper of Jesus was written by Paul. In First Corinthians 11:23–26, Paul speaks about it in order to help the community in Corinth overcome their internal disputes. People are meant to become unified and to achieve corporate salvation through the celebration of Communion. They all become the one "body of Christ." But those who exclude or discriminate against the socially disadvantaged eat unworthily and bring "judgment upon themselves." In addition, this passage of First Corinthians puts special emphasis on the remembrance of Jesus as a person and his story. This is manifest in respective commands that are linked to both the words of institution over the bread and the cup. Finally, contrary to the Gospels, Paul mentions that these events aim at proclaiming the death of Jesus and his return.

We have now compared the four New Testament texts that describe the Last Supper of Jesus (Matt. 26:26–29; Mark 14:22–25; Luke 22:15–20; 1 Cor. 11:23–26). Their most important passages shall, at this point, be presented side by side in a table. The texts are arranged in accordance with their relative age, beginning with First Corinthians.

Table 1:
Central New Testament Texts Concerning the Last Supper

1 Corinthians 11:23–26 (54–56 CE)	Mark 14:22–25 (approx. 70 CE)	Matthew 26:26–29 (approx. 85 CE)	Luke 22:15–20 (approx. 85 CE)
———	———	———	*Passover:* "For I tell you that I will not eat it again until it is fulfilled in the kingdom of God." *1ˢᵗ cup:* "For I tell you that from now on I will not drink of the fruit of the vine until the kingdom of God comes."

1 Corinthians 11:23–26 (54–56 CE)	Mark 14:22–25 (approx. 70 CE)	Matthew 26:26–29 (approx. 85 CE)	Luke 22:15–20 (approx. 85 CE)
Bread: The Lord Jesus . . . took bread, . . . "This is my body that is for you."	*Bread:* "Take; this is my body."	*Bread:* "Take, eat; this is my body."	*Bread:* And he took bread, . . . "This is my body that is given for you."
"Do this in remembrance of me."	———	———	"Do this in remembrance of me."
Cup: "This cup is the new covenant in my blood."	*Cup:* and they all drank from it. "This is my blood of the covenant, which is poured out for many."	*Cup:* "Drink from it, all of you, for this is my blood of the covenant, which is poured out for many for the forgiveness of sins."	*2nd Cup:* "This cup is the new covenant in my blood, which is poured out for you."

1 Corinthians 11:23–26 (54–56 CE)	Mark 14:22–25 (approx. 70 CE)	Matthew 26:26–29 (approx. 85 CE)	Luke 22:15–20 (approx. 85 CE)
"Do this, whenever you drink it, in remembrance of me."	——	——	——
"For whenever you eat this bread and drink this cup, you proclaim the Lord's death until he comes."	"Truly I tell you that I will not again drink of the fruit of the vine until that day when I drink it anew in the kingdom of God."	"I tell you: I will not again drink of this fruit of the vine until that day when I drink it anew with you in my Father's kingdom."	*(prepended, see above)*

These texts are the basis of the actual words of institution used in our churches today. However, these texts differ from one another, and so our various ways of celebrating Communion are not entirely identical with any one of them. Our Communion liturgies can, therefore, be understood as compilations or syntheses of the biblical texts.

The Last Supper in the Gospel according to John

Aside from the passages examined above, there is another notable text in the New Testament that deals with the Last Supper, although in a different manner. While the Gospel according to John (written ca. 90–95 CE) does tell the story of Jesus, including his passion and crucifixion, it does not explicitly mention the Last Supper. Instead, we read in John 6:1–15 that shortly before the Passover feast, Jesus and his disciples went to a mountain, being followed by many people—about 5,000 men. There was not enough to eat although a child had brought five barley loaves and two fish. Jesus took the loaves and said prayers of thanksgiving before giving the bread out to the people who were camped around him. It is noteworthy that the Greek verb for "to give thanks" is *eucharizein*, from which we derive the English word "Eucharist." In the story in John 6, all the people ate until they were full, and yet there were still leftovers to fill twelve baskets.

Later that evening, Jesus performed his miraculous walk upon the sea (John 6:16–21). The next morning the people once again crowded around Jesus and followed him. Jesus said to them, "You follow me not because you have seen signs, but because you ate of the bread and were filled" (6:26). Then he gave a long speech in which he twice referred to himself as the bread of life (6:35, 48). Jesus continued:

> "I am the living bread that came down from heaven. Anyone who eats of this bread will live forever; and the bread that I will give is my flesh for the life of the world." Then the Jews argued among themselves, saying, "How can this man give us his flesh to eat?" So Jesus said to them, "Very truly, I tell you, unless you eat the flesh of the Son of Man and drink his blood, you have no life in

you. Whoever chews my flesh and drinks my blood has eternal life, and I will raise that person up on the last day." (John 6:51–54)

It is difficult to understand these words as anything other than a sort of commentary on the Last Supper. They contain no indication of how Jesus actually conducted the Last Supper; this has been reported by Mark, Matthew, and Luke, as we have seen. But these words in John's Gospel offer important clues as to how the consumption of the "flesh" and the drinking of the "blood" of Jesus are to be understood. Here, though, we have an obvious problem: Jesus presents himself as the "bread of life" and "living bread," and then he says that those who eat of it will live forever. But how can a living person like Jesus be eaten? The answer that Jesus gives does not really help to clarify this point: how is it possible to consume the flesh and blood of someone who is alive?

In order to understand the meaning of these words, it is helpful to read some of the chapters before the speech of Jesus. It turns out that they repeatedly contain statements of Jesus that cause confusion and misunderstanding among his audience. There is, for example, the scene of the so-called "cleansing of the temple," which, in John's Gospel, is found at the beginning of the ministry of Jesus (John 2:13–25). Here Jesus speaks of the destruction of the Temple at Jerusalem while he was standing in front of it; moreover, he says that he will raise it up again in three days (2:19). This statement also caused confusion, which is why John provides his readers with some further explanation: "But he was speaking about the temple of his body" (2:21). So Jesus used the word "temple," but by this word he really meant his own body, and the destruction and recreation of it refers to his coming crucifixion and resurrection. What Jesus said is to be understood as *symbolic* or *allegoric*. Those who wanted to take his words literally, then, thought that the word "temple" referred to the actual building in Jerusalem in front of which Jesus was standing; they, however, did not understand his true meaning.

We see a comparable sort of passage in chapter 3. Nicodemus, a Pharisee and leader of the Jews, came to Jesus and asked him questions. Jesus answered him, "Very truly, I tell you, without being born from above, no one can see the kingdom of God." Nicodemus said to him, "How can anyone be born after having grown old? Can someone enter a second time into the mother's womb and be born?" (John 3:3–4). Here, too, Jesus wanted to explain something by using a symbolism, namely that of birth. Nicodemus, however, failed to understand him because he took the symbolic phrase of Jesus literally. Naturally, an adult cannot be born for a second time. But Jesus meant this in a different sense; he spoke about the start of a new, spiritual existence (3:8), which begins with baptism (3:5).

And if this were not clear enough, the next chapter of John's Gospel features yet another related scene. (We could perhaps comment that John used a method back then that is well known today from radio and TV commercials. Here, too, individual advertisements can be run repeatedly, and sometimes with slight variations, until the audience has accepted the "message.") This time Jesus was traveling through Samaria and met a woman by a well. He said to her that he was able to give her living water (John 4:10). Once again his words were met with incomprehension; the woman maintained—perhaps even with something of a sneer—that Jesus had no bucket (4:11). Yet here again, Jesus was not to be taken literally. He had not spoken of the mere physical substance of water; the "living water" was rather a symbolic expression for the good news that Jesus brought, which gave people new life.

Three scenes in the beginning of the Gospel according to

John are therefore similar to one another regarding a specific aspect: Jesus spoke of his body as being the temple; he said that an adult must be born anew; and he said that he could give living water. His words were misunderstood in all three cases by those who attempted to take them literally. And in all three cases, the key to unlocking their actual meaning was symbolic interpretation. As stated, it is helpful to consider these three scenes if we want to understand the words of Jesus in John 6 about the "bread of life." For here again, a literal interpretation of his words led to a misunderstanding; a person cannot, of course, give away his own flesh to another as bread to eat. Here, too, we find that the chewing of the flesh and the drinking of the blood of Jesus convey something else in a symbolic fashion. They signify rather the repeated or continuous study of, and meditation upon, the words, life, and mission of Jesus. These are the kinds of things we have to "chew on." They signify what the Christian church does every Sunday in its preaching office when the story of Jesus is told and retold and interpreted for the congregation. Because of this task, people start to believe in Jesus. In fact, the feeling of being "full" and faith are explicitly linked in John 6:35: "Jesus said to them, 'I am the bread of life. Whoever comes to me will never go hungry, and whoever believes in me will never be thirsty.'" In this way, Jesus is the bread that feeds hungry people. In another speech, Jesus connects faith and hearing his words; whoever has such faith has eternal life (John 5:24). Finally, it may be mentioned that the Gospel according to John introduces Jesus as the incarnate "word" (Greek: *logos*, 1:1–14).

If the words of Jesus and his story become the basis of faith and life, and if Jesus is this very word, then Jesus is the "bread" which "nourishes" the hungry. In the Christian Church and in theology today, the term "real symbol" is being used to designate this idea. The connection with the rest of the mission of Jesus is found before all else in the miracle of the multiplication of the loaves in John 6. The other such gospel miracles and the accounts of the Last Supper belong together.

I noted above that the Gospel according to John tells the story of Jesus and yet omits any account of the Last Supper proper—that is, the words of institution and the breaking of the bread and distribution of the wine are not described. This is all the more striking in that this Gospel does provide a detailed description of the final meal of Jesus with his disciples, which he celebrated in anticipation of his imminent death (John 13:1–20). Here, Jesus washed the feet of his disciples. The acts of service and humility, which in this account are so striking, are in a certain sense concordant with the allegory of the bread: Jesus served his people and in this way he gave them not only a new source of power, but also worthiness; and he made them into a new human community. In Jesus, God drew near to this world and to humans. God's grace and love for the entire world became visible in Jesus. His humble behavior was truly paradigmatic: "I have set you an example that you should do as I have done to you" (13:15). Here, then, lies the real ground for the salvation of humanity, and herein lies the reason why it is indispensable to read this special story of salvation. And this is the reason to read the Gospels even today during Christian worship, for they tell of how God's people become "saved."

Conclusion: Many of the words Jesus spoke were not meant to be taken literally. They were primarily to be understood as symbolic or emblematic. That goes also for his statement in John 6 that he was the bread of life. When Jesus called upon his listeners to chew his flesh and drink his blood, he also spoke figuratively. He suggested that people are always to think about him who became human and dwelt upon this earth for their sake. In his words and in the message of his life and death, God's salvation of humans is especially visible. That is true also for the miracle in which Jesus was able to feed many people with only a little food. It is striking, nevertheless, that the Gospel according to John does not feature any account of the Last Supper proper. Instead, the selfless love of Jesus and his readiness to serve are illustrated by means of a different story: he washes the feet of his disciples. This story sets an example of true humility for all humans.

Summary: The Last Supper in the New Testament

The Christian celebration of Communion goes back to the last supper Jesus ate with his disciples. We have now reviewed and compared the most important texts of the New Testament on this theme (Matt. 26:26–29; Mark 14:22–25; Luke 22:15–20; 1 Cor. 11:23–25; also Luke 24:13–35; John 6:22–59; 13:1–20). The essential information is as follows: Jesus gave bread and wine to his disciples at a final supper. He also spoke a blessing, a prayer of thanks, and the so-called "words of institution." According to the latter, the bread represented his "body," which was "given for you," and the wine represented his "blood of the (new) covenant," which was "poured out for many."

Jesus also conveyed that he was about to eat his last meal and anticipated his death. He nevertheless concluded with the prospect that there will be life after death. His words suggest, therefore, that the atmosphere of the Last Supper was characterized by both sorrow and hope.

The oldest texts concerning the Last Supper are found in Paul's First Letter to the Corinthians and in the Gospel according to Mark. The passages in the Gospels according to Matthew and Luke were written later; they continue to expound upon the basic information found in the earlier two texts (i.e., Matthew's version strengthens the hortatory character and inserts mention of the forgiveness of sin by the blood of the covenant; Luke's version emphasizes the Passover feast and features the unusual order *cup—bread—cup*). Only in Mark's Gospel, the word of institution pertaining to the cup is spoken after the disciples drank the wine. These words interpret this event not before it occurs, but in retrospect.

Thus, the New Testament texts that relate to the Last Supper are different, yet in essence they all tend toward the same meaning. In the texts of the Gospels of Mark, Matthew, and Luke, the Last Supper is the last meal that Jesus ate with his disciples. It has the character of a symbolic testament that conveys what Jesus did for humans in his life. This becomes clear when Paul explains the Last Supper in First Corinthians 11:23–26 in order to help the Christian community in Corinth overcome their inner divisions. The celebration of Communion is the event where the people of the congregation were supposed to meet and be united as the "body of Christ." In this way, the purpose of Communion was to render visible crucial aspects of the mission of Jesus on this earth.

Chapter 3

THE MEANING OF
THE LAST SUPPER

The effect of the Lord's Supper is peacefulness it provides within because we all sin but are forgiven and blessed.

—*Lorrie H.*

We are remembering the sacrifice of our Lord's body and blood, shed for our salvation. It draws us together back into one body cleansed and ready to glorify God in service to others.

—*Anonymous*

I n this chapter, we shall discuss in detail different aspects of the Last Supper or Communion that emerge from the study of the foundational New Testament passages. In doing so, we shall explore what the breaking of the bread and the drinking of the blood of the new covenant mean. We shall also examine the question of whether the Last Supper is a Passover feast and if the death of Jesus can be understood as atonement or as a sacrifice.

One Meal—Different Names

What is the meaning of the meal rite with bread and wine? Perhaps we should change this question slightly: What *are* its *meanings*? This meal has and had more than one meaning. Consider Christmas time: For most people today, it is a festive occasion for the mutual exchange of gifts. As such, Christmas functions as an indicator of social relations. Gifts are an expression of friendship; their exchange shows kinship ties and interpersonal relations. However, committed Christians often consider such an interpretation too superficial and commercial; after all, Christmas is still the festival of the incarnation of God. The particular circumstances of this birth demonstrate in a very special way that God chose those who were weak and rejected in this world. Today, therefore, Christmas has different meanings for different people.

This is also the case with the Last Supper or Communion. The different meanings of this celebration are, first, manifest in the variety of names for it that have always existed side by side within the Christian church. Second, there is the more general consideration that a certain celebration can be understood quite differently by different participants. Especially during celebrations that are periodically enacted, many participants readily recollect general rules of conduct since they follow them. On the other hand, they are often not aware of the deeper sense or origin of the rite.

So what is this celebration called nowadays? Reflect for a moment: which terms do you know, or which names are used in your church? Even within a single Christian denomination or congregation, different names are used. Here are a few common ones:

The Last Supper: This term is particularly common among Protestant Christians. It is coined after the circumstances of the historical incident. According to the sequence of events during the passion story, Jesus met with his disciples to consume his last meal before he was arrested, sentenced, and crucified. According to Mark 14:17, this happened in the evening; hence the meal is known as "supper." Paul refers to the "night" when Jesus was betrayed (1 Cor. 11:23) and later to a "supper" (v. 25).

The Lord's Supper: This term (Greek: *kyriakon deipnon*) occurs in First Corinthians 11:20. It is coined after the fact that Jesus, who is the "Lord" (Greek: *kyrios*), invited his disciples to this meal and spoke the blessing (Mark 14:22). According to Jewish customs, he took on the role of host of the meal. In so far as Jesus is the Son of God, the divine Father, the disciples—and afterwards all Christians—are understood to be the guests of God, the "Father" of all.

Eucharist: Today particularly Roman Catholic Christians use this expression. It is derived from the Greek word *eucharistia*, which means "thanksgiving." The word "Eucharist" refers literally to the thanksgiving that Jesus said during his Last Supper. In our investigation of the texts in the New Testament relating to the Last Supper, we saw that minor differences exist as to the exact moment when Jesus said this. According to Mark 14:23 and Matthew 26:27, thanksgiving is said over the cup, whereas according to First Corinthians 11:24 it is said over the bread; and according to Luke 22:17 and 22:19, it belongs to the first cup (of two cups) as well as the bread (see Table 1 on pp. 35–37). In the early Christian book "The Teaching of the Twelve Apostles," the Greek word *eucharistia* appears as the official designation for Communion (Did. 9:1, 5).[12] Therefore it is clear that the word *eucharistia* was already common in the 2nd century CE.

Breaking of the Bread: This expression is best known from its appearances in the Acts of the Apostles (2:42, 46; 20:7). It is peculiar because it refers only to the bread and not to wine. However, we saw already in the story of the disciples on the road to Emmaus that the breaking of the bread alone can reference the rite in its entirety and serves to remember and recognize Jesus (Luke 24:13–35). By contrast, there is no New Testament reference to the Last Supper that mentions the cup by itself without reference to the bread. Therefore the expression "breaking of the bread" can be understood as an abbreviation for the Last Supper, which early Christians usually celebrated with both bread and wine. Still today, some non-denominational Christian churches prefer to use the term "breaking of the bread."

(Holy) Communion: This term, too, is rather current among Roman Catholic Christians. Moreover, Catholics celebrate "First Communion," the occasion on which

young Christians are first allowed to take part in Communion. The term "Communion" is derived from Latin and essentially means "community" or "sharing." It might refer to First Corinthians 10:16: "The cup of the blessing that we bless, is it not the communion of the blood of Christ? The bread that we break, is it not the communion of the body of Christ?" It refers, at the same time, to the characteristic action of sharing bread within a community.

Love feast: This word occurs in Jude 12. The Greek word is *agapai*, the plural of "*agape*," which means "love." The term "love feast" conveys in a unique fashion that the highest Christian ideal is at the very center of the celebration with bread and wine: the love that became visible in the life and death of Jesus.

(Holy) Mass: This expression is almost exclusively used by Roman Catholic Christians. It is derived from the Latin term *missa*, which actually means "mission" or "sending." On the one hand, it refers to the Communion, on the other hand, it also refers to the entire Christian worship service. Thus, it is clear that the Communion truly presents the apex of worship.[13]

Synaxis: This word is Greek and means "unification." Therefore it is more or less equivalent to the term "Communion." The term *synaxis* is especially customary in Eastern Orthodox Churches but remains largely unknown to Christians in the Western churches.

Divine Liturgy: Orthodox and Catholic-Oriental Churches use this term to designate specific Eucharistic liturgies from the 4th and 5th centuries CE, which they still use today.

As I mentioned above, many Christian churches celebrate a rite with bread and wine as the climax of their worship services. They do however use at least nine different terms for this celebration. As we have seen, three of these—"Lord's Supper," "breaking of the bread," and "love feast"—are already featured in New Testament texts. "Eucharist" and "Communion"—and indirectly also *"synaxis"*—occur there, too, but are not known yet as technical terms for the celebration with bread and wine. Therefore, the New Testament lacks one standard expression. As a consequence, the Christian church has never settled upon any fixed term in the 2,000 years of its development. It was far more important to keep on celebrating the rite—and to allow the church to be formed by it.

While examining all these terms, we may wonder why the church still uses such old and traditional expressions derived from Greek or other languages. Does this practice not complicate worship services more than necessary? That may well be. These foreign expressions demonstrate, nonetheless, that the church attends to its long tradition with care. As one aspect of such care, the church continues to use at least the most central or important terms in the language of its tradition.

Before I present even more such examples of church terminology, it should be mentioned that even in everyday speech, we use many words that are old and derived from foreign languages. Thus, for example, the English word "automobile" is derived from the Greek word for "self" (*autos*) and the Latin word for "moving" (*mobile*), respectively, to describe a mechanical device that moves all by itself. Many other technical or political expressions are also borrowed from these two classical languages, for example the words "politics," "television," "democracy," or "president."

Such a reliance on tradition can especially be found in old proverbs. We still say, for instance: "He's champing at the bit," even though we could modernize and adapt this saying thus:

"He's revved up and ready to go." Yet we tend not to do this. Hence, outmoded words are still used in old proverbs although they would no longer be employed at any other occasion.

HISTORY AND BACKGROUND:

Traditional Expressions in the Church

Someone who participates in a Christian worship service today is perhaps surprised by some of the expressions used there—or will simply not understand them. Why are words like "amen" or "hallelujah" used, and what does *kyrie eleison* really mean? Do such words perhaps have some sort of magical power?

The answer to these questions lies in the long and eventful history of the Christian church. Most of these words have been used in worship for a long time. It is therefore a token of recognition of this long past that such words have not simply been forgotten. These words are moreover derived from other languages: *kyrie eleison* is Greek and means "Lord, have mercy"; "*Christe eleison*" means "Christ, have mercy"—the liturgies of some churches thus translate these expressions immediately. The word "amen" is Hebrew and means "truly," "verily," or "so it is." And "hallelujah" means "praise God" (and is similar to the Arabic expression *alhamdulillah*). It is evident that the history of the Christian church did not begin in English-speaking nations, but in different cultural environments using different languages. On account of this, we also find in such "church lingo" various Latin and even Aramaic words ("hosanna" means "please save us"). Such terminology, therefore, has nothing to do with any magic. A long and rich history lives on in it until this day.

Conclusion: Christian denominations and churches use very different terms for the rite with bread and wine. These different expressions indicate that this rite, while being of central importance, has had diverse interpretations. Some of these expressions are derived from various texts of the New Testament itself. Today the church continues to use such old and traditional terms out of respect for, and attachment to its long history.

The Last Supper—a Ritualized Meal

The New Testament and the church have deployed various terms to refer to the celebration that we study in this book. Yet there is one sure thing that remains simple and unaltered: Jesus established a rite with bread and wine, the fundamental components of the Last Supper. For ages past, bread and wine were basic staples of the human diet. Moreover, the texts of the New Testament explicitly state that Jesus distributed bread and wine to his disciples and asked them to eat. Thus Jesus introduced a ritualized meal with basic staple foods. He added specific words that indicated that the rite had a deeper meaning beneath the surface of words. However he associated this meaning with the simple activities of eating bread and drinking wine. Later disputes over what the Last Supper could mean mostly arose from arguments over the meaning of these words. Yet there is almost never any controversy about the simple gestures of sharing bread and wine.

It is worth considering that the Last Supper of Jesus was essentially a ritualized meal, and that Christians, whether they celebrate Communion daily or weekly or four times a year, are just as well celebrating such a ritualized meal. After all, every person is able to relate to such an event in some way because a meal is one of the most basic human experiences. Since their first moments on earth, humans have taken sustenance from food, and will continue to do so for the rest of their lives.

Because a meal is such a basic experience of life, it is a wonderful starting-point for communicating a deeper level of symbolism. Second, a meal is fundamentally open to very different interpretations. Every person can say what a meal means to him or her. For some it may be important that there is something delicious to eat; for others who are starving, a meal gives strength and guarantees survival. Still others appreciate a meal because the processes of preparing and eating often occur in good company and provide an experience of community. People probably gather for meals most often as a family although sometimes also with friends or colleagues at work. The social aspect of the Communion will be further discussed later on (see pp. 100–108). For the moment, it is important to know that everyone can understand a gesture with bread and wine. And since Jesus spoke words that clarified this gesture and conveyed a specific interpretation, such words were accessible to everyone. All interpretations of these words are therefore possible. Since the Last Supper is a ritualized meal, there is really no false interpretation so long as this rite is understood to be a meal. That should be emphasized here before we delve into further special aspects of Last Supper and Communion below.

Conclusion: Jesus instituted the Last Supper as a ritualized meal. The most important elements are the distribution of bread and wine. Since every person regularly takes part in meals, and since bread and wine were the staple foods of past days, the symbolism of the Last Supper is basically accessible and comprehensible to all people.

The Last Supper and the Passover Meal

> The Last Supper is chiefly a meal commemorating the suffering and death of Jesus. As such, the details of it contain many symbolic meanings, which unfortunately are not yet clear to me.
>
> —*Hartmut Sander*

We have seen that the core of the Last Supper consists of a ritualized meal with bread and wine. Apart from that, the New Testament texts dealing with the Last Supper contain a wealth of information regarding bread and wine and how they were understood by Jesus, the early church, and by extension, how they are to be understood by us.

One of the last things that Jesus did before his crucifixion was to ask his disciples to prepare a Passover meal (Mark 14:12–16). The passion of Jesus occurred during the time of a well-known Jewish festival that combined the Passover and the Festival of Unleavened Bread. Both were folk festivals of the early Jews. This means that a great many meals were prepared, and all participants ate and drank well. Today we understand Communion as a rather scanty meal—nobody really fills his or her stomach. The actual Last Supper at which Jesus shared bread and wine with his disciples was probably not opulent either. In the Gospel according to Mark, the Last Supper was only the conclusion of a richer feast. This meal is the Passover meal for which the tradition required that a lamb be prepared (14:16).[14] As previously mentioned, Jesus and his disciples were busy eating before or during the "Last Supper" according to Mark (see above, p. 18). The Apostle Paul, too, recognizes the Last Supper of Jesus as the final part of a more bounteous and longer meal (see above, p. 29).

But Passover was more than just a good meal with food and wine. It also had important religious and political significance for Judaism that many people today are not aware of. To better understand the framework of the Last Supper or Communion, therefore, we shall explore the origins of Passover. This requires a study of certain Old Testament texts.

The Passover festival was one of Israel's traditional celebrations. According to the narrative in Exodus 12, it was a family feast.[15] The father of each household organized the celebration and could invite his neighbors for a common celebration (Exod. 12:3–4). Central to this ritual was the remembrance of the exodus from Egypt and the rescue of the people of Israel from bondage (12:25–28). According to the tradition, one would hear repeatedly of God saving the people of Israel from slavery, oppression, and domination. The powerful nation of Egypt had exploited the Israelites for its own pompous building programs (1:8–14).

And yet there was another reason why Passover was important to the Jews. After the exodus, their ancestors arrived in a new land promised to them by God and found a new identity. Passover is the festival of the first step on their journey. It reminded the Jews later on that they had become an independent and free nation. This background of the Passover festival was especially meaningful during the day of Jesus since Palestine was governed by the Romans. The residents of this area were, therefore, living under foreign occupation. Of course, some Jews at the time were also proud to belong to the great Roman world Empire. Yet it was quite clear that the small province of Judea, where the city of Jerusalem was located, was being exploited just like the other Roman provinces that comprised the region of Palestine. Here and elsewhere, many people suffered under the oppression of Rome and its heavy taxes and tributes.

HISTORY AND BACKGROUND:

Taxes and Tribute in Ancient Palestine

The Roman Empire had a huge administrative system. It built roads, public buildings, temples, and of course supported an army. All that cost a lot of money. Extra-biblical sources indicate that in order to cover these costs, Rome levied taxes on people, land, and goods. In Palestine as in other areas of the Roman Empire, two kinds of tributes were levied, direct and indirect. The direct taxes were levies on crop yields and head taxes. They were collected by local Jewish authorities of the province under the oversight of the Roman procurator. The indirect taxes included tolls for using streets, bridges, ferries, city gates, and markets; these were mostly collected at these various sites.

Due to Roman oppression, the Passover feast had an immense political significance for the Jews. Many left their native villages to make a pilgrimage to Jerusalem and celebrate. People traveled together and met others in their capital city. There, the Jews also used this occasion to recruit men for military purposes, though this was illegal in the eyes of the Romans. For this reason the commemoration of the salvation from Egyptian slavery, which was so characteristic of Passover, always included the possibility of political unrest or even the beginning of guerilla movements and uprisings. This made the Roman occupiers nervous. So they watched Jesus carefully to see if he would present himself as a political or religious leader for the Jews. The charge of Jesus of Nazareth as "King of the Jews" (Matt. 27:37; Mark 15:26; Luke 23:38; John 19:19) tells us that the Roman occupying force eventually accused him of high treason and executed him for political motives.

The Passover festival, considered as the background to the Last Supper, was a very explosive and controversial occasion. Emotions were mixed; on the one hand, there was festive joy and national pride, and on the other hand, there was fear of political unrest. Such a Passover festival is mentioned in Mark 14:12-16. Allusions occur also in the actual references to the Last Supper which contain the key word "remembrance." It appears once in Luke 22:19 and twice in First Corinthians 11:24-25. At a traditional Passover feast, the Israelites remembered their journey out of Egypt. For this purpose, children were supposed to ask their fathers about the reason for the celebration, and the fathers would recount the old exodus narrative (Exod. 12:25-28).

But there was more to the people's remembrances. As stated above, special words that interpreted the eating of a meal as the commemoration of salvation were especially associated with the celebration of Passover. The eating itself symbolized something important. During the night of Passover, the entire meat of the Passover lamb was roasted over the fire. It was to be eaten "in a hurry," so everyone was ready to go "with loins girded, shoes on your feet, and your staff in hand" (Exod. 12:11). The *mazzot* breads, which were unleavened breads, alluded to this underlying haste; the Israelites had to eat bread not yet properly leavened. Later the preparation of the Passover lamb and the *mazzot* bread facilitated each in their own way a living reenactment of the exodus.

When early Christians celebrated Communion, they likewise met with the goal of commemoration. And the consumption of food had symbolic value as well. But there are differences. In distinction to the Jewish Passover, Christians are not commemorating a saving *event* so much as a *person*, Jesus, who brought salvation. Another difference between the Last Supper and the Passover lies in the nature of danger and where the danger is coming from. The Israelites lived in a hostile environment and had to sustain themselves against the overwhelming power of the Egyptians. When Jesus celebrated the Last Supper with his disciples, he also found himself in a hostile situation caused by religious and political authorities. But the danger came not exclusively from the outside, from "the other;" it came from the inner circle of Jesus as well. Judas Iscariot, one of the twelve disciples, had betrayed Jesus (Mark 14:10–11). And even Peter denied him a short time later (Mark 14:66–72). Properly understood, the Last Supper commemorates liberation from both inside and outside threats. Yet in the case of Jesus, liberation did not include bypassing death. Liberation occurred instead three days later in the resurrection. Accordingly, the liberation that early Christians celebrated was victory over death.

Conclusion: The Last Supper ritual that Jesus celebrated with his disciples took place during the Passover festival. It was situated in the context of a Passover meal and probably occurred as the final part of a more sumptuous feast. Passover was a traditional Jewish family feast that centered on the commemoration of salvation from Egyptian slavery. The very eating of the food itself was symbolic—the way the food was prepared and consumed was an essential part of the commemoration. At the time of Jesus, Palestine belonged to the Roman Empire, and its inhabitants had to pay high taxes. Passover therefore stirred up nationalist sentiment in many Jews, and this made the Roman occupying authority nervous. The communal food of the Last Supper was also a symbol of the commemoration of liberation. Its focus was the person of Jesus who brought salvation from danger. Yet salvation for Jesus became manifest not through liberation from imminent death, but through resurrection and a definitive victory over death.

The Meaning of the "Blood of the New Covenant"

[The Eucharist is] a remembrance of what Christ has done for me: dying, forgiving in love. No one should be denied if they know Jesus. I "feel" a new beginning each time I go, a cleansing.

—*Eva J. Elke*

By now, we have outlined the festive and ritual context of the Last Supper. We had also set out to understand that the Last Supper is in essence a simple meal with the staple foods of bread and wine. Accordingly, the symbolism of the Last Supper is accessible to every person. And due to the context of the Passover feast, it has to do with the remembrance of salvation.

Yet Jesus pronounced what we today call the "words of institution" when he first offered the bread and the cup to his disciples. According to the earliest texts in the New Testament, these words are, "this is my body," spoken over the bread (Mark 14:22) and, over the wine, "this is my blood of the covenant, which is poured out for many" (Mark 14:24) or "this cup is the new covenant in my blood" (1 Cor. 11:25). We also noticed that, in the Gospel according to Mark, Jesus spoke the word of institution pertaining to the cup after the drinking of the wine. With these words, he gave hints as to how he understood this short, ritualized meal and how he wanted others to understand it. On the following pages, we shall therefore study these words in detail. I would like to begin with the word of institution spoken over the cup.

When Jesus offered the cup filled with wine, he spoke of a "covenant" or "new covenant." What does that mean? Do you generally use the word "covenant" in your own church? As far as I am aware from visiting various Protestant, Roman

Catholic, and Orthodox churches, the word "covenant" is invoked only during Communion. This lingo is not typically found outside of the church, so many people are confused about its meaning. Therefore, it can be difficult to make sense of Jesus' expression "this is my blood of the covenant." But when we don't understand the meaning of these important words, we no longer understand central aspects of the Last Supper or Communion. Hence, we shall explore their origins in this chapter. Like our previous reflections on the Passover, this requires a study of Old Testament texts.

When Jesus used a word like "covenant," he didn't have to explain it. His fellow Jews understood what he was talking about. On many other occasions, Jesus said things that were difficult to understand, such as his various parables (Mark 4:1–9) for which he offered explanations later on (4:10–20). But the words of institution refer to traditional ideas, which were probably known to his listeners. The concepts were easy for them to understand.

This is quite simply because Jesus was citing a very important text from the Torah, the Holy Scripture of the Jews. And it is likely that Jews knew this text very well. It is about the journey out of Egypt when God led the Israelites through the wilderness. They were on their way to the Promised Land where they were supposed to reside one day. Much time passed before they arrived, and they faced many dangers and conflicts. There was, however, a significant stopping point along the journey, where the Israelites camped for a long time—Mt. Sinai. This was no ordinary place. The Torah presents it as the mountain of God. People were able to encounter God at this place. Moses had led the Israelites here, and according to the biblical account, he climbed this mountain. God gave him the Ten Commandments (Exod. 20:1–17) there and various other laws (Lev. 26:46).[16]

Mt. Sinai is particularly where God sealed a covenant with the Israelites. It is this covenant that Jesus referenced during the Last Supper. The covenant at Mt. Sinai was necessary since the Israelites were not the people of God per se. To the contrary, God is described as being so holy in the Torah that the Israelites were not even able to approach the mountain (Exod. 19:20–25; 24:1). The Israelites were considered sinners, and in a way, the covenant was God's response to human sin.

In today's culture, we may struggle with the fact that, in the Bible, a human being is not simply described as good and without fault. The church speaks of sin, but is that really necessary? We all try to live upright lives, of course. Nevertheless, we must recognize not all is well with our world and our personal lives. To speak of human sin means in some degree simply to be honest with ourselves. In spite of our best efforts and highest ideals, people are not perfect, and the reality of our daily lives remains unpredictable. Consider these verses by Lothar Zenetti:

> *We know it enough*
> *that real life is tough*
> *and fragile and frail*
> *and love too may fail*

This poem captures, in part, what the Bible means by sin. It should be mentioned that biblical texts feature no precise definition of sin. We are rather given hints as to its meaning from very different Old and New Testament texts; the reconstruction of the actual understanding of sin that informs each of them remains the task of the interpreter. In this book, a comprehensive definition cannot be given. Nevertheless, I would like to propose an outline of basic aspects. Generally, sin is a fundamental separation between humans and God, and is often the consequence of disobedience to God's commands.

These two dimensions coincide in the story of the first sin (or the Fall). After Adam and Eve had eaten the fruit of the tree in spite of God's commandment, they were forced to leave Paradise and God's presence (Gen. 3). Sin always has negative consequences for individuals or for the community, and in the worst case, it leads to death (4:1–16). Christian authors wrote later that all people stand under the power of sin (Rom. 3:23; 1 John 1:8). In the end, only God can liberate humanity from the sphere of its power. This insight is emphasized in Christianity. Paul wrote that God justifies humans freely and through grace (Rom. 3:24). Jesus even told the parable about the Pharisee and the tax collector. The tax collector trusted in God's grace and was justified while the Pharisee, who had fulfilled several of God's commandments but showed contempt for others, was not justified (Luke 18:9–14).

When God's people wandered through the wilderness, sin was the reason the Israelites were not permitted to approach God. They were not even allowed to touch the mountain of God (Exod. 19:23)—at least not initially. But God prepared a surprise for the Israelites, the surprise of the covenant. For this covenant, Moses built an altar at the foot of Mt. Sinai (24:4). Then he had bulls offered as sacrifices on this altar.

> Moses took half of the blood and put it in basins, and half of the blood he sprinkled on the altar. Then he took the book of the covenant and read it to the people. They said: "All that Yahweh has spoken we will do, and we will be obedient." Moses took the blood and sprinkled it on the people, and said: "See the blood of the covenant that Yahweh has made with you in accordance with all of these words" (Exod. 24:6–8).

This passage describes the covenant that Yahweh made with Moses and the Israelites. This covenant had two components. First, Moses read ethical precepts that God had given to him beforehand (Exodus 24:3–4). The story tells us explicitly that the Israelites accepted them. Then Moses sprinkled the blood of the sacrificial animals upon the Israelites. Both components are therefore different, and yet belong together and complement each other. The biblical text indicates this by their similar names: "book of the covenant" and "blood of the covenant." At the Last Supper, Jesus referred to this passage concerning the covenant at Sinai. When he said, "this is my blood of the covenant" after (or before) he gave the cup filled with wine to his disciples, he recited the words that Moses spoke at the covenant at Sinai according to Exodus 24:8. As stated above, this text belongs to the Torah, the most important part of the Holy Scriptures of Judaism. Even today, many Jews know the entire Torah by heart. And we may suppose that during the time of Jesus, many could recite this text from memory as well. People would have understood that Jesus was referring to the words of Moses when he spoke of the "blood of the covenant."

What did Jesus mean when he named his own covenant after the covenant at Sinai? That covenant between God and the Israelites was the fundamental paradigm for interpreting the drinking of the cup of wine at the Last Supper rite. One who knew what the "blood of the covenant" had affected at Sinai understood also what the "blood of the covenant" signified at the Last Supper. Thus today, we must first of all try to understand the covenant at Sinai. Then we will also understand the Last Supper. So let us turn once more to the narrative of the covenant at Sinai.

I said already that the Israelites were initially disconnected from the holy God. Human sin separated them from God.

Nevertheless, the Israelites bound themselves to follow God's commandments, which Moses read to them from the "book of the covenant." In this way they renounced their sins and resolved to accept ethical responsibility. This was the first component of the covenant between God and Israel.

Moreover, Moses sprinkled the blood of the sacrificial animals over the Israelites. This was the second component of the covenant. Just what might this action mean? Such a scene appears strange to us nowadays since sacrificial rituals are no longer carried out in our churches or in other venues of our western culture.[17] But to understand the covenant of Moses at Mt. Sinai and why Jesus quoted it during his Last Supper, we need to explore sacrificial rituals in the Old Testament. I therefore invite you to study texts in the Bible that many Christians have never read and that few pastors or priests of the Christian Church ever preach sermons on. But many of these texts are at the heart of the Torah and belong to the oldest portions of the Bible. And they deal with a topic that is usually much misunderstood today. Thus we shall first study sacrificial rituals in general and then focus on blood rituals that will help us to understand the covenant at Mt. Sinai.

Sacrificial rituals were part of everyday life in the world of the Old and New Testament. Conducted throughout the ages, they were unquestioned elements of worship. Accordingly sacrifices are mentioned everywhere in the Old Testament as, for example, the sacrifice of Jacob (Gen. 31:54) or those of Elkanah and Hannah in Shiloh (1 Sam. 1). What is more, the Old Testament contains lengthy guidelines for the correct performance of ritual sacrifices (Lev. 1–7). The book of Leviticus as a whole principally contains numerous descriptions and directives for every conceivable sort of ritual offering. This includes, above all, detailed lists with instructions for yearly festivals and holidays. For such occasions, the Israelites made pilgrimages to the central temple, where further ritual sacrifices were presented (Lev. 23; Num. 28–29).

Even later, at the time of early Christianity, sacrifices were still common practice. When Jesus healed a leper, he told him that, for his purification, he was to go and offer the proper sacrifice as prescribed in the Torah (Mark 1:40–45). And in the famous Sermon on the Mount, Jesus used the example of a person coming to offer a sacrifice in order to explain the importance of reconciliation with one's neighbor to obtain forgiveness from God (Matt. 5:23). This means that he did not fundamentally challenge ritual sacrifices. Finally, in the day of Jesus, the Greeks and Romans had their own temples and sacrificial rituals, and in fact the same could be said for all peoples who were living in the ancient Near East, for example the Babylonians, Egyptians, Hittites, and the Phoenicians.

Ritual sacrifices may be quite unfamiliar to us today; but as we have seen, they were common at the time of Jesus and long before then. The question remains, however: Why did people offer sacrifices? There were, in any event, different occasions. First, sacrifices were an expression of reverence and thanksgiving when people came to the temple in order to worship God. In doing so, people acknowledged that, in the end, they owed their prosperity to God. And in nomadic societies, such material wealth was chiefly measured by the size of herds. Thus in so far as people sacrificed one of their animals to God, they gave back a part of their prosperity. For this reason, even today the collection of donations in churches is still called "offering" or "sacrifice." These collections resemble the practice of ritual sacrifice in some fashion. We have obtained prosperity and give back some of it. Because such prosperity is nowadays measured in terms of money, we drop cash into the collection plate or basket—

or we pay via automated money transfer from our bank account.

Second, ritual sacrifices made food available. All the materials which people were allowed to sacrifice at the temple were edible items. The livestock that was prescribed for ritual sacrifices (Lev. 1:2; 22:17–20) was otherwise meant for human consumption. No game or non-domesticated animals could be offered. It was also permissible to bring grain mixed with oil as cereal offerings (Lev. 2); this mixture was finally to be salted (2:13). All of these things were everyday food staples and as such acceptable at the temple.

What then became of these materials? A portion of all such ritual sacrifices was offered up to God; it was to be burnt on the central altar in front of the temple. (The altar at the Jerusalem Temple is depicted above, p. 45.) The idea was that, through this fire, the offering would be "transported" to God, who then accepted it. In the priestly texts of the Old Testament, the sacrificial rituals are described in detail; and in reference to the fire, the stereotypical comment is found: "for a pleasing odor to Yahweh" (Exod. 29:18, 41; Lev. 1:9, 13, 17; 2:2, 9, 11; 3:5, 16; 4:31; 8:21; Num. 15:3, 10). So people back then thought that God would smell the sacrifice, even if this notion is somewhat alien to modern people.

Moreover, a portion of all ritual sacrifices—with the exception of the burnt offering described in Leviticus 1—was given to the priests who maintained the temple and organized the divine worship there. They received, for example, certain meat portions as their sustenance (Lev. 7:28–36). Finally, the persons who brought the sacrifices to the temple also received their own meat portion (7:11–21). They typically ate it during a jovial festival. At any rate, it had to have been consumed on the third day from the date of the sacrifice at the latest (7:17). One should recall that, in those days, there were no refrigerators, so meats would quickly spoil.

Sacrificial rituals had numerous functions. To return once more to the comparison with offering plates in today's churches, we might call to mind that many people continue to benefit from this modern "sacrificial" practice as well. For one thing, these offerings support the work of churches. For another, many worthy endeavors are financed by means of these funds. Such collection of money is rightly called a "sacrifice," for its purpose is comparable to the function of ritual sacrifices of ancient times.

We have not yet explored one particular function of such sacrifices, namely the "blood of the covenant." It was first mentioned at the covenant at Mt. Sinai. Blood was always held in great awe in Judaism, and there were laws that prohibited the consumption of animal blood (Lev. 3:17; 7:26–27; Deut. 12:23). These laws were still observed in early Christianity (Acts 15:20) and, later on, even in Islam. What was the reason for this respect and awe? It is based on the idea that the life of all creatures is in their blood, as Deuteronomy 12:23 states explicitly. A related passage goes even further connecting blood with atonement—and atonement is an effect of ritual sacrifice: "For the life of the flesh is in the blood; and I [God] have given it for you upon the altar to make atonement for your lives; for it is the blood that makes atonement, by reason of the life" (Lev. 17:11).

What was the blood of the sacrificial animal used for? Biblical texts provide a range of different purposes. It was, for example, used to consecrate candidates for the priesthood by sprinkling it on them (Exod. 29:19–21; Lev. 8:23–24). During the ceremony of the "Day of Atonement," the Jewish Yom Kippur, the blood of sacrificed animals was sprinkled in the sanctuary and applied to the altar (Lev. 16:15–19). In both cases, the intended effect was similar: the blood consecrated—which means it "made holy"—the candidates for the priesthood and the sanctuary. Before this ritual ceremony, the candidates were unclean due to sin just like any other person; after contact with sacrificial blood, they were holy. Now they were permitted to perform their priestly service in the sanctuary and before the holy God. Moreover, the sanctuary itself was initially considered unclean and had to be consecrated through the sacrificial blood. Only after all of this was accomplished would the holy God of Israel reside in this place.

In the Old Testament, the effect of such acts of consecration was called "atonement." The aforementioned passage in Leviticus 17:11 connects the elimination of sin with blood and life. In the background is the idea that sin represents death. But as the symbol of life, blood is able to remove sin. Hence, when the blood of sacrificial animals is brought into contact with people, they are rendered "holy." They can now draw near to God and need not fear anymore.

The nature and purpose of sacrificial blood and its effect help us to understand the ritual that Moses performed at Mt. Sinai. To repeat briefly what occurred there, the Israelites had arrived at the mountain, which was held to be God's place of residence; yet on account of their sins, they were not permitted to draw closer. Moses then read from the "book of the covenant" and sprinkled sacrificial blood, which he called the "blood of the covenant," over the Israelites (Exod. 24:6–8). How does this story continue?

> Then Moses and Aaron, Nadab, and Abihu, and seventy of the elders of Israel went up, and they saw the God of Israel; and under his feet there was something like a pavement made of sapphire stone, clear as the sky itself. And he [God] did not raise his hand against the leaders of the people of Israel; they saw God, and ate and drank (Exod. 24:9–11).

Here we witness a real happy ending! Not only the prophet Moses, but also some of the Israelites could climb the mountain and see God there; and this is stated twice, in verses 10 and 11. After that, they held a party, eating and drinking before God. The Bible really states this!

Note the following aspects from this astounding scene. First of all, the Israelites ate meat on the mountain that came from the animals sacrificed earlier according to Exodus 24:5. These sacrifices are called "offerings of well-being" or "fellowship offerings" in different Bible translations. This meat was to be consumed by those who offered the sacrifice.

Second, the Israelites were made holy. This is the effect of the two components of the covenant. One component is the "blood of the covenant," which Moses had sprinkled on the Israelites. This blood represents life and had the power to purify people from sin, which is the liability of death. In this way, the Israelites were purified, although they had not always displayed appropriate behavior before. Because the symbol of life removes the liability of death, the Israelites could now celebrate before God. In keeping with the sense of the passage of Leviticus 17:11, they were made holy like the priests who served God at the sanctuary. The effect of this ritual action is similar to the self-commitment of the Israelites and their willingness to follow the instructions given in the "book of the covenant." Both components of the covenant sanctified the Israelites in different ways. Both components contributed in their own way to the "covenant" which God made with Moses and the Israelites, the covenant that enabled the Israelites to become God's people. I shall summarize its most important aspects in the following table.

Table 2:
The Covenant at Mount Sinai

Two Components	"Book of the Covenant" (Exodus 24:7)	"Blood of the Covenant" (Exodus 24:8)
Precondition	The Israelites are separate from God	
Actions	Moses reads the book to the people; they accept the laws (Exodus 24:7)	Sacrifices are offered; Moses sprinkled the blood on the people (Exodus 24:5, 8)
Effects	Sin is being eliminated; the Israelites are now holy (consecrated)	
Consequences	The covenant between the Israelites and God is now established (Exodus 24:8); the Israelites climb on Mt. Sinai; they see God and eat and drink in front of God (Exodus 24:9–11)	

Few people nowadays know this surprising text of the Torah. This could explain why even regular church-goers, or those who are well versed in the Bible, are often convinced that, according to the Old Testament, no human could ever see God. Yet according to Exodus 24:9–11, Moses, the future priests Aaron, Nadab, and Abihu, and also seventy of the elders of the people climbed the mountain "and saw the God of Israel."

Even if most Christians today are no longer familiar with this surprising passage, it was certainly well known to Jews at the time of Jesus. Perhaps many of them even knew it by heart. At the celebration of the Last Supper, Jesus could therefore quote the words "blood of the covenant" from this text. The companions of Jesus would have immediately known what he referred to. Furthermore, while most Christians nowadays have no clue about sacrificial rituals or related blood rituals, the disciples of Jesus could have possibly seen them with their own eyes at the Temple in Jerusalem just the day before the Last Supper. This center of the Jewish religion was still standing during the lifetime of Jesus—it was not destroyed until after his death, in the year 70 CE when the Romans sacked Jerusalem during the Jewish War. The disciples were thus familiar with both the Old Testament passage that Jesus referred to and ritual sacrifices themselves.

What then did Jesus mean to say when he spoke of the "new covenant in my blood"? And how did his companions understand these words? The wine that Jesus offered them represented his own blood according to his word of institution that, in turn, drew on well-known expressions from the Old Testament (Gen. 49:11; Deut. 32:14). It corresponded to the blood of the sacrifices offered at Mt. Sinai. In addition, the effect of the Last Supper was in some way similar to the covenant at Sinai. Of course, at the Last Supper the wine was not sprinkled onto the disciples. But in so far as they drank from the cup, they still came into direct physical contact with the wine. When Jesus indicated after they drank that the wine was now "the new covenant in my blood" (1 Cor. 11:25) or "my blood of the covenant" (Mark 14:24), he implied that their sins had been forgiven. Those who drank from the wine were made pure. They became like the Israelites who, according to Exodus 24, climbed up Mt. Sinai and were able to see God. They were made holy like priests serving before God. Another early Jewish text, which is not in our biblical canon, calls both wine and bread "most sacred" (*Testament of Levi* 8:5). Such sacredness is transmitted to the partaker of the meal of Jesus. And finally, a "covenant" was sealed. The people who took part in the meal then belonged to God and were considered God's people.

The motif of the "covenant" was very well known in Judaism. Throughout the long and alternating history of this religion, it conveyed that God always intervened in all moments of crisis to stand by his chosen people. Accordingly, the Bible repeatedly mentions instances of sealing covenants, such as these three:

1. A popular prophetic book in the Old Testament refers to the special blood rite that Moses performed at Mt. Sinai: "As for you [daughter Jerusalem] also, because of *the blood of my covenant* with you, I will free your captives from the waterless pit" (Zech. 9:11). Apparently, this text is imparting the hope that God will finally bring salvation at a time of dire straits. In doing so, the "blood of the covenant" is designated as the feature that motivates God to think of the people in need. And when this happens, God will save them—in this instance literally out of a pit in which they had been dying of thirst.

2. Another prophetic text speaks even of a "new" covenant and connects it with the forgiveness of sins: "Behold, the time is coming, says Yahweh, when I will *make a new covenant* with the house of Israel and the house of Judah" (Jer. 31:31). This covenant is not the same as the earlier one that God made with the people to lead them into the Promised Land. The Israelites had not entirely

adhered to the earlier covenant (31:32). Therefore, the new covenant will be different; it will be engraved into the human hearts. Then there will no longer be any doubt that the Israelites belong to God (31:33).

3. Finally, early Christian texts also refer to the covenant at Mt. Sinai between God and the Israelites. In the anonymous New Testament text "To the Hebrews" (usually called the "Letter to the Hebrews"), the author attempts to explain the effects of blood rituals:

> For when every commandment of the law had been declared by Moses to all the people, he took the blood of calves and goats, with water and scarlet wool and hyssop, and sprinkled the scroll itself and all the people, saying, "This is *the blood of the covenant* which God ordained for you." And in the same way he sprinkled with the blood the tent and all the vessels for worship. Indeed, under the law, almost everything is purified with blood, and without the shedding of blood, there is no forgiveness of sins. (Heb. 9:19–22)

This text also quotes the passage from Exodus 24:8 about the blood of the covenant. It makes the inference that the various blood rituals in the Old Testament purify in a similar fashion. The fact that this was explained in Hebrews 9 indicates that details about blood rites were already unfamiliar to some people towards the end of the 1st century CE when this text was written. After all, the temple in Jerusalem had been destroyed almost three decades earlier, and since then, people could no longer perform sacrificial rituals. Therefore, they were already making an effort to explain how human sin was to be forgiven in the context of sacrificial rituals.

Nowadays, it is still difficult to understand such rituals and their effects since we are not very familiar with their underlying biblical basis. Moreover, our worship practices differ from those in Judaism many centuries ago. Today we offer no more animal sacrifices in order to carry out rites of aspersion with their blood. As time passes, many customs and conceptions simply undergo change.

On the other hand, can we today even imagine that the drinking of wine is capable of wiping away sins? This idea, too, strikes us as somewhat strange. We can indeed no longer fully reconstruct and understand many of the customs and traditions that biblical texts describe or presuppose. To give a further example, in the liturgy of some churches, Christians respond to the exhortation "Lift up your hearts" with the words, "We lifted them to the Lord." What exactly does this mean? Are we literally moving upwards in worship or asked to stand straight? Or does this have something to do with our feelings, in as much as the heart is often considered to be the seat of the emotions? Ought we therefore try to "feel" God? Neither answer is correct. In antiquity, the heart was not considered to be the seat of emotions. People generally held it to be instead the seat of the intellect or understanding. Hence, the exhortation "Lift up your hearts" is a traditional appeal to focus one's thoughts on God.

This insight renders another biblical expression understandable. In the Gospel according to Mark, the miraculous story about the multiplication of the bread (Mark 6:30–44) is followed by the narration of how Jesus first astounded his disciples by walking on the sea and calming a dangerous storm (6:45–52). The conclusion to this story simply reads, "For they [the disciples] did not understand about the loaves, but their hearts were hardened" (Mark 6:52). In this final passage, it is clear that the reason for the disciples' failure to learn anything from the multiplication of the bread was due to their "hardened hearts." Underlying this statement is the implication of the ancients' idea of humanity. Hence, this story is about the disciples' lack of comprehension.

Such traditional conceptions or expressions remain as a part of our worship today. But when we inquire into their exact meaning, they can strike us as odd. In order to understand them, we must make an effort to explore and comprehend them as they were understood by the ancients. As stated above, Hebrews 9:19–22 is a New Testament text that attempts to clarify older Jewish rituals and their effects for an early Christian readership. Throughout history, those interested in older traditions and ideas have been confronted with the task of needing to appropriate older customs through research and teaching.

Conclusion: In this chapter we considered the meaning of the cup with wine at the Last Supper. We thoroughly investigated the words of institution that Jesus spoke after his disciples had drunk: "This is my blood of the covenant." These words are not self-explanatory to modern listeners. Yet in Jesus' time, Jews would have recognized a quotation of a well-known and central text from the Torah about the covenant at Mt. Sinai that God sealed with Israel. It also refers to blood rites in the context of sacrificial rituals that were still customary back then. In the covenant at Sinai, the blood that Moses sprinkled on the Israelites had an important role. It was the "blood of the covenant" that symbolized life and was considered holy. By means of sprinkling this blood, the Israelites were consecrated and made holy. The immediate consequence was that they were entitled to climb up Mt. Sinai where they saw God and celebrated. Through the covenant, they became God's people.

When Jesus celebrated the Last Supper with his disciples, wine took the place of blood. Yet the wine had a function similar to the sacrificial blood used at the covenant at Sinai. The disciples were consecrated by drinking this wine. Their sins were forgiven, and they became God's people. In this way, Jesus established his "new covenant" with them. The poet Lothar Zenetti conveys similar ideas in the following poem:

> *This is my blood, poured out for you,*
> *   it stains a cross-shaped steeple,*
> *The covenant, forever true,*
> *   makes all of you God's people.*
> *The blood of grapes you pour for us*
> *   a cup with wine of sorrow*
> *Unite us, Lord, in faith and pass*
> *   your love on us tomorrow.*

Suggestions for Workshop 1:

What does the "blood of the new covenant" mean?

1. *Please read* Exodus 24:1–11; Exodus 29:19–21; Leviticus 14:10–20. You can also act out these scenes by having different groups play one of these Bible texts.

2. *Please discuss* first: What ritual elements do these biblical texts have in common? What do the texts say about effects of the rituals?

3. *Please discuss* then: Do these Bible texts help you to gain a better understanding of the account of the Last Supper in Mark 14:22–25 or of the celebration of Communion in your church?

The Death of Jesus and Atonement for Sins

Like "covenant," the word "atonement" is also a traditional concept that Christianity inherited from Judaism. Do we know what atonement means? Here again, modern people may have a gap of understanding. Today, the English term "atonement" is mostly used in the field of jurisprudence. There it refers to indemnification that compensates for acts of wrongdoings. So when we hear about atonement in theological formulations, judgments and punishments easily come to mind. If we think in only these terms, God may appear as a tyrant, a despot who judges, condemns, and demands recompense for human misconduct. So how would people understand the atonement of Jesus in such a context? They would most likely describe it as a recompense that Jesus had affected for humanity or as vicarious punishment.

It is important, however, for us to understand that such conceptions of punishment or recompense do *not* form the basis of atonement at the covenant at Mt. Sinai or in the context of sacrificial rituals. I pointed out above that the blood rites in the Old Testament have a different meaning. The blood of sacrificial animals is holy and removes human sin since it represents life. The Torah described this conceptual connection as "atonement" (Lev. 17:11; see above, pp. 67–68), and this concept of atonement was familiar to early Christians. Back then, therefore, Christians understood the concept of "atonement" *not* in the sense of punishment or recompense. A brief overview of the New Testament texts that mention words like "atonement," "place of atonement," and so on, will clarify this.

a. A Christian confession was formulated at a very early date. It essentially says that God presented Jesus as an "atonement" or rather as a "place of atonement" as proof of divine righteousness. Around the year 56 CE, Paul wrote his letter to the Romans and referenced this confession. He expanded it slightly in order to explain the ways and means by which Jesus redeemed sinful humanity: "They [the sinful humans] are now justified freely by his grace through the redemption in Christ Jesus, whom God put forth as atonement [or: a place of atonement] through faith in his blood" (Rom. 3:24–25). It is of importance for our discussion that both the early Christians and Paul understood atonement as being effective through the blood of Jesus because it had the power to eliminate sins.

b. The First Letter of John describes Jesus in a similar manner as "atonement for our sins, and not for ours only but also for the sins of the whole world" (1 John 2:2). Earlier in this text, the "function" of this atonement has been specified: "and the blood of Jesus, his [God's] son, cleanses us from all sin" (1 John 1:7). As stated above, this is not about vicarious punishment but about purification.

c. A lengthy passage in Hebrews 9–10 deals particularly with atonement rituals. These two chapters start with a description of the ministry that the Jewish high priests had to perform on Yom Kippur, the "Day of Atonement." At the center of attention are sacrificial blood rites which the high priest performed annually according to the instructions in Leviticus 16:14–19. These prescriptions are recapitulated in Hebrews 9:7: "But only the high priest [goes] into the second [part of the sanctuary] once a year, and not without blood [from sacrificial animals] that he brings for himself and for the sins committed unintentionally by the people." Hebrews 9:11 suggests that the mission of Jesus should be understood in analogy to such high priestly tasks, although Jesus is said to have entered into a heavenly sanctuary. This in turn is said to have been superior to the earthly sanctuary in which the high priest performed his duty. A further difference is the eternal forgiveness of sins that Jesus is said to have acquired, since he entered into the heavenly sanctuary "through his blood" (9:12). This lengthy passage finally offers an explanation of how this forgiveness is achieved: "For [already] the blood of goats and bulls and ashes of a heifer, sprinkled upon those who have been defiled, sanctify so that their flesh is purified. Then how much more will the blood of Christ, who through the eternal Spirit offered himself without blemish to God, purify our conscience from dead works to serve the living God!" (9:13–14). Once more, the elimination of sins is described as purification, and similar arguments occur later in the text as well (9:21–22; 10:19–22).

d. Approximately at the time of composition of the First Letter of John and the writing "To the

79

Hebrews," Judaism produced the text known as the Fourth Book of the Maccabees.[18] This work describes a moving scene in which Eleazar and his sons die as martyrs. With a view toward his imminent death, Eleazar says in his farewell speech that his blood may be "a means of purification" (4 Macc. 6:29).

These texts consistently assume that blood has special power. They relate blood with purification, the forgiveness of sins, and atonement. This conception is derived from sacrificial rituals of the Old Testament, and it also informs the "new covenant in my blood" that Jesus established at the Last Supper. Jesus foresaw his imminent death and wanted to convey its special meaning to his disciples— and perhaps also to everybody else. In order to do this he gave a cup with wine to the disciples, and he accompanied this act with a well-known Torah passage about the covenant of Moses at Mt. Sinai. So this was the paradigm for the atonement of his death: his blood had the power to eliminate human sin.

Conclusion: According to various texts in the New Testament, the death of Jesus affects atonement. It would nevertheless not be appropriate to describe atonement in terms of punishment or judicial recompense. Instead, sacrificial rituals of the Old Testament yield the conception that animal blood had the power to eliminate the sins of people. Biblical texts describe this process explicitly as purification. When during the Last Supper Jesus introduced the "new covenant in my blood," he was referring to atonement in the sense of such purification. Therefore, wine that represents the blood of Jesus effectively removes sins when people drink it.

Was the Death of Jesus a Sacrifice?

> To him shall endless prayer be made,
> And praises throng to crown his head;
> His name like sweet perfume shall rise
> With ev'ry morning sacrifice.
> —*2ⁿᵈ stanza from church hymn no. 434*
> *"Jesus Shall Reign" by Isaac Watts (lyrics)*
> *and John Hatton (music), from*
> *the hymnal* Evangelical Lutheran Worship

In the previous chapter, we studied several sacrificial rituals in biblical texts and discussed their purpose or effects. Now we shall tackle the question: Can the death of Jesus on the cross be understood as a sacrifice? We all know the reference to Jesus as a sacrifice from the proclamation of various Christian churches. Also the idea that Communion is to be understood as a repeated sacrifice is sometimes attested: during worship, the priest is thought to sacrifice Jesus, who is present in bread and wine, on the altar. This sacrifice is supposed to be understood in analogy to the sacrifice of Jesus on the cross. Is his death, therefore, the same as a sacrifice in the Old Testament?

In the passion stories of the New Testament, however, things appear somewhat differently. According to these texts, Jesus was officially executed on a cross by the Roman occupying authority in Palestine. The placard affixed to the cross read: "The King of the Jews" (Mark 15:26; Matt. 27:37) or "Jesus of Nazareth, King of the Jews" (John 19:19). It indicated that Jesus was condemned as a pretender to the title of Messiah. In concrete political terms, this meant that he was executed for high treason and political subversion. The Roman Empire prescribed the death penalty of execution by crucifixion for such offenses.

HISTORY AND BACKGROUND:

Crucifixion and the Inscription on the Cross

The crucifixion was an especially gruesome and humiliating form of execution. It involved tying or nailing the condemned to a wooden pole, which may or may not have had a lateral crossbeam for the arms of the convicted. Usually death would come after many hours or even days. This form of execution was widespread in Greco-Roman culture, and it was frequently practiced in the Roman Empire.

A wooden placard featuring an inscription would often be placed on the cross. In Latin it was called *titulus crucis,* or "cross title." It generally stated the reason for the condemnation of the convicted—in the case of Jesus, treason or sedition. According to the accounts of the Gospels, the title on the cross of Jesus was written in Hebrew (or Aramaic), Latin, and Greek (John 19:20), so in the two official languages of the Roman Empire and also in the local tongue. The reason for the condemnation of Jesus could be read by onlookers (or it could be read for them aloud by the *literati* or scribes, as literacy was not too common in those days). For such onlookers, the drawn-out torment and cruel death of the crucified person were meant to serve as a terrifying warning.

Was such a shocking penal event being described as a "sacrifice" back then? Interestingly the passion narratives of the New Testament never feature this word. Ritual sacrifice was something quite different from the scene of someone who had been judicially executed. In order to clarify the difference between the two, let me briefly recapitulate some central aspects of ritual sacrifices as they were stated above (pp. 64–67): Sacrificial rituals were widespread both in the cultures from which the Old and New Testament emerged, and in the religions and cultures surrounding them. Sacrifices were offered because people wanted to give thanks to God or when they had special requests. Moreover, people hoped that their sins would be forgiven. Comestible items were sacrificed, namely livestock or grain. A part of these was burnt on the altar and so given to God while another part was for the priests. Finally, after the ritual, sacrificial meat was often available for consumption by the community that had gathered to celebrate.

So much for a brief review of sacrificial rituals. What can we add at this point? Depending on the reason for offering a specific type of sacrifice, the "mood" of the ceremony could vary greatly. Most sacrifices were offered in festive ceremonies at the temple. A rather detailed description of a sacrificial festival is featured in Second Chronicles 29:20–36. At the start of his reign, Hezekiah (725–697 BCE), the new king of Judah, reorganized the administration and the sacrificial worship in Jerusalem. In doing so, the priests, the Levites, the people, and the king himself gathered at the temple. Musicians played cymbals, harps, lyres, and trumpets (2 Chron. 29:25–26). During the sacrificial rituals, the "Song of the Lord" (29:27) was sung in addition to psalms of David and Asaph (29:30). Such information conveys that the general mood at this festival was cheerful and happy. The text repeatedly states that "They sang praises with joy, and they bowed down and worshipped . . . and Hezekiah and all the people rejoiced because of what God had done for the people" (29:30, 36). We must likewise imagine that the atmosphere was happy and celebratory during, for example, the Jewish Festival of Weeks (Lev. 23:15–21; Deut. 16:9–12) or during the Festival of Booths (Lev. 23:33–43; Deut. 16:13–15), which are more or less comparable to our own holiday of Thanksgiving.

Yet I explained that in the culture of the Old Testament, ritual sacrifices could be offered for various reasons. While some sacrifices were offered during festive occasions, sadness and repentance dominated the Day of Atonement, or Yom Kippur. Accordingly, the entire population observed a fast and did not work (Lev. 16:29–31; 23:26–32). This underlying mood was due to the fact that, on Yom Kippur, the sins of the people were removed by means of rituals performed at the temple. Furthermore, the sanctuary itself was being purified, as is indicated in Leviticus 16:33: "and he [the high priest] shall make atonement for the Holy of Holies, and he shall make atonement for the tent of meeting and for the altar, and for the priests and for all the people of the community he shall make atonement."

The reason for sadness and repentance on Yom Kippur is not because ritual sacrifices as such were considered sad or threatening events. But such a conclusion is often drawn because of the assumption that sacrifice is all about animal slaughter. This is not correct, however. I mentioned already that ritual sacrifices were to be given to God according to the regulations of the Old Testament. By means of the fire on the altar, they were "transported" to God (see above, p. 66). Therefore, cereal offerings, which consisted of grain, oil, and frankincense (Lev. 2), were also counted as ritual sacrifices. These substances could, according to the Jewish and Christian worldview, not be "slain." The fact that such non-animal offerings were sacrificed allows us to conclude that, even according to Old Testament ritual laws, it was not the act of killing or slaughter per se that determined if something was a ritual sacrifice or not.[19] Therefore we should not jump to the conclusion that a ritual sacrifice was necessarily a violent and grim affair. The biblical examples I have cited above show that, to the contrary, the mood during sacrificial festivals could be very cheerful and happy.

In the Bible, sacrifices are not invariably considered to be connected to a tragic fate. The biblical use of the term "sacrifice," therefore, is somewhat different from how the word is generally understood today. We often employ the term "sacrifice" when we speak about wounded or slain soldiers. The word then conveys the noble motives of those who went on a dangerous mission. But at the same time, it necessarily has a tragic, almost threatening connotation. This is, however, entirely foreign to the biblical conception of sacrifice; in the various texts of the Old Testament, the term "sacrifice" is never used to describe dangerous or tragic circumstances or instances of murder. When, for example, David was ready to gladden the sagging spirit of King Saul with his harp music, the King was gripped with envy and wanted to kill him. The text in First Samuel 18:10–11 mentions that this happened repeatedly—David therefore knew that he was in danger. Nevertheless, he remained in the royal palace in order to serve Saul. In describing what happens in this narrative, we might say in modern terms that David was ready to "sacrifice" his own life. It is significant, however, that the word "sacrifice" is not used in the biblical account. It simply means something different in the Old Testament.

The situation was quite the same when the conflict between David and Saul gradually escalated to the point where David was forced to flee. He was then temporarily supported by Ahimelech and the priests of Nob (1 Sam. 21:2–10). When King Saul heard of this, he interpreted this help as an expression of disloyalty to himself. He therefore seized not only the priests of Nob, but also all the other inhabitants of Nob and had them put to death (1 Sam. 22:6–19). Nowadays, we would, once more, use the term "sacrifice" in a double sense to refer to those who suffered this tragic fate; Ahimelech and the priests of Nob provided well-intentioned help in order to preserve the safety of a fugitive, David. Yet since they might have perceived that conflict was at the basis of David's escape, they were willing to "sacrifice" their own safety and perhaps their lives. On the other hand, Saul was willing to "sacrifice" many innocent people because of his jealousy and maybe also because of intentions to solidify his political power. Yet once more, the biblical texts do not use the term "sacrifice." This is because here as elsewhere, the concept of "sacrifice" in the Old Testament refers first of all to specific sacrificial rituals. And these rituals, as stated above, are in no way practiced always under the auspices of death or tragedy. Sacrificial rituals were occasions in which people communicated with God; they could equally be imbued with a happy as well as a solemn spirit. In modern usage, however, the word "sacrifice" is used to refer to loss, casualties, or some other such tragic fate.

It is important to be conscious of these different uses of the term "sacrifice" before we return to the question of whether the death of Jesus on the cross was a sacrifice or not. This question can be answered differently depending on the different connotations of the two definitions of sacrifice. In accordance with the *contemporary usage* of the term, the politically motivated execution of Jesus can absolutely be described as a "sacrifice." This label is then applied to mean that it was and is tragic when anyone who lives out a mission of altruism and non-violence is killed by ruthless forces operating on behalf of the Empire. The *biblical* term "sacrifice," however, conveys something different—and is therefore never applied to Jesus in the passion stories.

Nevertheless, elsewhere the New Testament does describe Jesus as a "sacrifice" and indeed uses terminology otherwise used for describing sacrificial rituals. One such example is Ephesians 5:1–2: "Therefore be imitators of God, as beloved children. And walk in love, just as Christ loved us, too, and gave himself for us as an offering and sacrifice for God as a pleasing odor." What does this phrase mean? The concluding words "as a pleasing odor" are a citation from Old Testament texts on sacrificial rituals. I explained already that this expression refers to the process when fire consumes the offering upon the altar; the understanding was that this fire "transported" the offering to God. The expression itself implies that God accepts the sacrifices offered by the people (see above, p. 66). When such terminology from the Old Testament is applied to Jesus in the New Testament, then it is meant as a metaphor or emblematic expression—after all, according to the passion story, Jesus had not been burnt by priests on an altar in front of a temple.

Is it perhaps possible that these terms refer exclusively to the death of Jesus or to his willingness to die? Beyond doubt, such an attitude would be truly exemplary. It would, however, fail to explain how such an attitude could serve as the model for the behavior that is recommended in these paragraphs of the Letter to the Ephesians. Chapters 4–6 of Ephesians list many examples of proper behavior that are recommended to Christians. For example, "Let no evil word come out of your mouths, but only what is helpful for building others up" (4:29); "be kind and compassionate to one another, forgiving one another" (4:32); "do not get drunk with wine" (5:18); "talk to one another in psalms and hymns and spiritual songs, sing and make music to the Lord in your heart" (5:19). For this kind of behavior, people were supposed to follow the example of Jesus, namely his love, his commitment, and his "sacrifice." So now the question is: Could the death of Jesus or his willingness to die be a concrete example for such behavior? The answer is no. It's more likely that the various graphic details of the entire life of Jesus were thought to serve as example—it rendered the love of God particularly visible. Hence the life of Jesus is the example for the daily behavior of Christians.

In a similar fashion, Paul asks the congregation in Rome "to present your bodies as a living sacrifice, holy and acceptable to God" (Rom. 12:1). He immediately explicates what he means with these words. Christians in Rome are asked to focus their renewed minds upon "what is good and acceptable and perfect" (12:2), put their various talents and gifts to work (12:3–8), be joyful and patient with perseverance in prayer (12:12), overcome evil with good (12:21), etc. Once more, the term "sacrifice" does not refer to negative things, but to positive things that make life worth living and special and are expressions of the love of one's neighbor.

In addition, if we construed the sacrificial metaphor in Ephesians 5:2 to refer exclusively to the death of Jesus, then it would remain rather mysterious why this biblical phrase includes the words "as a pleasing odor." In sacrificial rituals of the Old Testament, these words generally convey that God accepted what humans offered. This means for the metaphor in Ephesians 5:2 that the life of Jesus was fully accepted by God despite his shameful death on the cross. This life, then, brought salvation for the world.

The matter is presented somewhat differently only in the New Testament text "To the Hebrews," which was written several decades after Paul's letters. There Jesus is also described as a sacrifice. Unlike in Ephesians 5:2, the actual death of Jesus is now central: "And just as human beings are destined to die once, after which is the judgment, so Christ was sacrificed once to bear the sins of many and will appear a second time, not to deal with sin, but to save those who are expecting him" (Heb. 9:27–28). Again, the meaning of this metaphor is that Jesus brought salvation for the world. Central to the conception in Hebrews is the power of the blood of Jesus to remove human sin. This is analogous to the Old Testament concept of atonement according to which purification and forgiveness of sins are affected through blood, which contains life (see above, pp. 77–78).

The same idea underlies the "new covenant in my blood" pronounced during Communion.

Conclusion: Is the death of Jesus to be understood as a "sacrifice"? Or does the Last Supper mean that Jesus was sacrificed? According to the texts of the New Testament, the Roman occupying authority condemned Jesus out of political motives, namely for sedition, to die on a cross. Such a terrifying penal sentence had little in common with the festive ritual sacrifices at a temple. Therefore neither the passion narratives proper nor the accounts of the Last Supper nor any New Testament Gospel describe Jesus as a "sacrifice" in the sense of the Old Testament. In Ephesians 5:2, on the other hand, the entire existence and life of Jesus are described in metaphorical terms as such—and this means that his life was accepted by God and affected salvation for the world. In the writing "To the Hebrews" (also called the "Letter to the Hebrews"), the blood of Jesus becomes central to the discussion of sacrifice, for this blood is presented as having the power to remove human sin.

The Meaning of the Breaking of the Bread

The Catholics say that, in the Eucharist, God is embodied in the bread and wine. The Reformers say that Communion is a commemorative meal. For me there is no contradiction. God is always in all things in his Spirit, for he created all things and continues to be present in them. Thus when we hear, "This is my body," so he is from the beginning onwards. Communion serves to remind me that God works in all things through Jesus Christ and also wants to say something particular to me today.

—*Klaus Busch (68 years old).*

The Lord's Supper is a visible means of grace enacted in Christ; it is where a real presence of Christ is realized.

—*Marc Jerry (37 years old).*

In my opinion, Communion is a remembrance of Jesus Christ; it should always remind us of what he has done for us.

—*Mareike Behrens (10 years old).*

We have seen that Communion is a simple meal at its core. Everyone can comprehend and appreciate it as such. The words which Jesus spoke over the cup of wine show, however, that Jesus himself provided some guidelines as to how this meal should be understood. He quoted a text from the Torah that was well known at the time, namely the text describing the covenant between God and Israel at Mt. Sinai (Exod. 24:8). In order to comprehend his interpretation, it is necessary for modern people to become familiar with the concepts of atonement and other rituals in the Old Testament. We have explored this in the preceding chapters.

Now the question arises, what does the breaking of the bread mean? The respective words of institution are given in Mark 14:22: "And when they [Jesus and his disciples] were eating, he took bread and after blessing it broke it and gave it to them and said, 'Take; this is my body.'" The Gospel author Luke later added the words, "that is given for you" (see above, p. 36). What might all of these words mean? Do they suggest that the bread had been miraculously transformed? Is the breaking of the bread, therefore, similar to the miracle at the wedding at Cana where Jesus turned water into wine (John 2:1–11)?

Such an interpretation is, however, unlikely in the passage of the breaking of the bread. First, in the entire scene it is obvious that Jesus is still alive and with his disciples. In view of this fact, could it be possible that the bread and wine that Jesus handed out to the partakers of the meal really somehow became his own flesh and blood? But this text is not about that. Specifically in the passage on the Last Supper featured in the Gospel according to Mark, which is the oldest of the New Testament Gospels, such an understanding is impossible. We have seen that, according to Mark 14:23–24, Jesus pronounced the word of institution pertaining to the cup only after his disciples had drunk the wine (see above, p. 16). This word can, therefore, be seen as a subsequent interpretation of the event of drinking. It is difficult, however, to construe it as an event that would have retroactively changed the substance or quality of what had been consumed previously.

Second, if such a miraculous transformation had been implied in the text of the Last Supper of Mark 14, then this would have been clearly indicated and in some fashion brought to the attention of the readers, just as the story of the wedding at Cana explicitly mentions the transformation of water into wine (John 2:9–11). In the passage of the Last Supper in Mark 14, however, there is no remark whatsoever of any sort of miracle or an actual transformation of bread and wine. Jesus certainly says while breaking the bread, "This is my body." Yet these words are uttered by Jesus who, first, constantly spoke in a symbolic or emblematic way (Matt. 16:5–12; John 4:5–14), and who was, second, fond of using parables (Mark 4:1–34; Matt. 13:44–52). Third, Jesus also said, "I am the bread of life" (John 6:35, 48) and "I am the living bread" (6:51), or "I am the light of the world" (8:12), "I am the gate for the sheep" (10:7), "I am the good shepherd" (10:11, 14), "I am the way and the truth and the life" (14:6), and so on. Yet, we do not assume that Jesus was actually transformed into a gate or a shepherd, etc.

All these motifs indicate in a comprehensive way who Jesus really was and what his actions in this world meant for humanity. These motifs are images or symbols. They indicate no more miraculous alteration than the words of institution in the context of the Last Supper. Consequently, the bread that Jesus blessed, broke, and gave to his disciples had not turned into his own flesh. What then could these words have meant? What does the gesture of the broken bread signify?

In order to answer these questions, let us follow the same method we used with the words spoken over the cup and look for similar phrases elsewhere in the Bible. This time we will mainly find them not in the Old Testament but in the New. It is particularly interesting that we find similar phrases near at hand; in fact, in the Gospel according to Mark itself, we actually find several of them. Attentive readers who have read this Gospel from beginning to end would recall the relevant passages. The miracle of feeding the masses or the miracle of the multiplication of the bread occurs twice before the story of the Last Supper, namely in Mark 6:30–44 and Mark 8:1–9. Concerning the feeding of the 5,000, we read, "Taking the five loaves and the two fish, he looked up to heaven, and blessed and broke the loaves, and gave them to his disciples" (Mark 6:41). And in the story of the feeding of the 4,000, we read, "Then he ordered the crowd to sit down on the ground. And he took the seven loaves, and after giving thanks he broke them and gave them to his disciples to distribute" (8:6). In both cases, there is an analogous narrative structure:

Bread (and fish) taken—blessing/thanksgiving spoken— bread broken—distribution to partakers.

This structure corresponds to Jewish meal customs that were observed at the time. It also underlies the narrative of the Last Supper. If we had read the Gospel according to Mark continuously, we would probably have noticed these repeated sequences right away.

HISTORY AND BACKGROUND:

How do Christians Read the Bible?

In contemporary Christian churches, biblical texts are read during worship. Some people also read the Bible at home. In many churches, it is a special reading habit to juxtapose individual passages from the Old and New Testament that correspond because of a particular aspect. This custom conveys that not only the New, but also the Old Testament is considered as holy scripture by the Christian churches. Both relate to each other and belong together. In the early days of Christianity, it was important to emphasize this because, at the beginning of the 2nd century CE, the church leader Marcion of Sinope (died 160) pushed for Christianity to distance itself fully from the Old Testament.

Nevertheless, in modern worship practice, a passage is seldom read in the context of its own chapter or even of the entire book. Therefore, its wider connections or the larger narrative arc are usually overlooked. Many people who follow this scheme of lectionary reading in our Christian churches are thus not aware that many passages of similar content do recur as, for instance, the two accounts of the miracle of feeding in Mark 6:30–44 and 8:1–9, or the three times when Jesus foretells his own suffering and death in Mark 8:31–33; 9:30–32; and 10:32–34. Moreover, it remains unnoticed that such individual passages often stand in a special context and broader connection with the text before and after them. Hence the scene when Jesus foretells his suffering and death in Mark 8:31–33 is in direct response to Peter's assertion that Jesus is the Christ (Mark 8:29). It is, therefore, worthwhile to read the books of the Bible from start to finish—back then, they were written for this very purpose!

It is also important to understand within its proper context the breaking and distribution of the bread that Jesus had blessed. The Last Supper has many clear and meaningful connections with the two miracles of feeding the crowds. What do these miracle stories mean, and how do they help us to understand the breaking of the bread at the Last Supper? In the Old Testament and in both early and contemporary Judaism, there was first of all the expectation that God's envoys, the prophets, could miraculously satisfy the hunger of many people by using very little food.[20] Jesus is presented as such a prophet in the stories of the multiplication of the bread, and it is to be expected that he must have special power and authority "from above." In light of this, the disciples should not have been surprised that Jesus, after multiplying the bread, presented himself as the Lord of natural forces—he could also walk on water and command the storm. Yet the disciples somehow did not see that the multiplication of the bread was supposed to make them aware of who Jesus was. Their lack of vision is acknowledged with an almost frustrated undertone: "for they [the disciples] did not understand about the loaves, but their hearts were hardened" (Mark 6:52).[21]

The two stories of the multiplication of the bread also demonstrate that Jesus had a concern for the poor. According to Mark 6:34 and 8:1, a "great crowd" came and surrounded him. Such words, as a rule, indicate simple people of low social standing. Jesus is particularly concerned with their needs, and so he dedicated his mission particularly to the suffering and outcast. Thus, he healed the sick (Mark 5:21–34; 7:24–30) and disabled (Mark 2:1–12; 7:31–37; John 9) and even brought the dead back to life (Mark 5:35–43; John 11:1–45); he saved a condemned woman (John 7:53–8:11) and forgave sins (Mark 2:5; Luke 7:47). Lothar Zenetti described this existential concern of Jesus for all humans with the following concise words:

The Meaning of the Last Supper

Who is Jesus for me? He is someone who is for me.
What opinion do I hold about Jesus? That he holds me.

The society Jesus lived in was full of poverty, misery, and bodily disability. These conditions were even considered the just punishment of God (John 9:2). Therefore, such people suffered from social stigma and ostracism as well as from their natural ailments. In contrast to this general attitude, Jesus maintained an entirely different position and dedicated himself to the "losers" of society. He gave them back their dignity in so far as he made possible their reintegration into society.

In the stories of the multiplication of the bread, hunger is understood as an allegory for human need. During the time of Jesus, nourishment was far sparser than in our modern Western world; it was, therefore, more important. In the Gospel stories, bread symbolized nourishment in general, but it could also represent that which people needed the most. During the life of Jesus—and incidentally even today in most places of our own world—a person's most obvious need was usually nourishment. For us in the modern Western world, this may be something else. What do we need the most? Human care and companionship? Time?

The Miraculous Multiplication of Time

And as he saw a large crowd
he had compassion for them,
and he began to teach them
about the irresistible love of God.

When it grew late, his disciples said to him:
Lord, send them away,
it is late, they have no time.

You give them some of that, he said,
give them of your time!

We don't have any time, they replied,
and what little we have is minute,
how could that be enough for so many?

But there was one among them who still had
five time slots available, not more, just in case,
and two half hours as well.

And with a smile, Jesus took
the five time slots that they had,
and both half hours in his hand.
He looked up to heaven,
gave thanks and praise,

then he gave the precious time
to his disciples to set before the large crowd.
And behold: It was minute, but the minutes were enough
    for all.
In the end, they filled twelve days
with what was left of all the time,
now that was not minute.

It is reported that they were amazed.
Because they realized that the impossible
is possible with him.

—Lothar Zenetti

A third aspect is that the first of the two stories of the feeding of the crowds stands in contrast to the immediately preceding narrative about the death of John the Baptist (Mark 6:14–29). The decision to murder John was also made during a meal, which was a banquet put on by King Herod "for his high officials and officers and the leaders of Galilee" (6:21). Important decisions are still made today at dinners and receptions, sometimes even decisions which determine the life or death of other people. The narrative sequence of the story of the death of John the Baptist (6:14–29) just before the feeding of the crowd (6:30–44) is an indication that grand and expensive banquets often cause doom and misery, whereas the simplest meals can bring life and blessings. The Last Supper stands in the tradition of the latter. However, in the Last Supper, blessing and doom are manifest simultaneously; it is a meal that establishes human community and affects the forgiveness of sins. Yet in so far as Jesus hints at the coming betrayal and disavowals of himself, it also contains an element of doom.

It is quite conspicuous how frequently the activity of Jesus occurs in the context of meals. The Last Supper is connected directly to the feeding of the crowds, but also stands in relation to all the other situations in the life of Jesus that revolved around banquets. These include the meal with "many tax collectors and sinners" in Levi's house (Mark 2:15–17), the anointing at Bethany (14:3–9), the invitation of Zacchaeus, the chief tax collector (Luke 19:1–10), and the wedding at Cana (John 2:1–11). In light of this, the Last Supper can be seen as the reference point of many of Jesus' parables dealing with meals, for example the parable of the "great dinner" (Luke 14:15–24). Likewise, the actual problem in the story of the prodigal son is the feast sponsored by the generous father in honor of the returning son (15:30).[22]

What do almost all of the New Testament stories about meals have in common? Let us have a close look at the people who met with Jesus and followed him. When we do, we are struck by what a motley crowd they made! Through faith in God and through baptism, a community is formed from many people of various backgrounds. Paul speaks of this fact later on: "There is no longer Jew or Greek; there is no longer slave or free; there is no longer male and female. For you are all one in Christ Jesus" (Gal. 3:28).

The reality that Jesus gathered very dissimilar people around himself is also visible in his disciples who formed his immediate entourage. For instance, Levi (or Matthew) the tax collector normally collaborated with the Romans (Mark 2:14; Matt. 9:9). There was Simon the Cananaean who was also named a "zealot" (Luke 6:15). He belonged to a Jewish group prepared to take up arms to fight against the Romans. Nevertheless, Levi/Matthew and Simon the Cananaean both followed Jesus. Apparently, the group Jesus led was no esoteric one, no hermetic or reclusive sect dedicated to secret teachings. It was rather an exoteric and overt group including some who aggressively sought to transgress accepted social boundaries. The Last Supper illustrates this before all else.

It was with such ideas of an open and inclusive community that Jesus set himself apart from the status-conscious and hierarchical society of his day. His teachings and his presence, as those of his disciples, must have appeared provocative. It was predictable that the conflict with larger society would escalate. To that extent, the crucifixion was foreseeable. Immediately before the Last Supper, Jesus foretold the betrayal that would lead to his arrest (Mark 14:17–21). The Last Supper itself was a celebratory feast and a foreshadowing of the grim death of Jesus at the same time. The breaking of the bread effectively represents this death. The bread of which Jesus said "this is my body" motivates the enduring, reverent memory of the life-giving history of salvation, in which Jesus made visible the grace and love of God for this world. In this sense, Jesus gave himself for others so that they may have life.

This commitment, devotedness, and surrender are alle-gorized in a unique way by the breaking, distribution, and consumption of the bread, and also by the drinking from the cup. On account of this, the Christian church is able to speak of the real presence of Jesus during the communion service.[23] In the words of Michael Welker:

> The identification with bread and wine expresses the creative surrender that occurs for the benefit of others, the creative, free process of putting oneself in the place of others. The bread that is being distributed during the Eucharistic meal celebration in remembrance of the surrender of Christ commemorates in a concentrated fashion the essence, the decisive aspect, and the truth of the person of Christ.[24]

The commemorative aspect of the representation may be due to the context of the Passover feast, in which the consumption of food was itself a symbolic component of remembering the delivery of the Israelites from slavery (see above, pp. 57–58).

Conclusion: In the breaking of the bread during the Last Supper, we see the convergence of the various miracles of feeding the multitudes and the numerous meal-scenes described in the Gospels. The breaking of the bread refers back to central events in the mission of Jesus. The scenes of the miraculous feeding of the crowds (Mark 6:30–44; 8:1–9) in particular show forth Jesus as God's envoy who cares for people in need regardless of their social backgrounds. Various other narratives of meals in the Gospels always convey that Jesus seeks the company of people who are considered sinners and who are socially ostracized. Some say today that Jesus clearly had a "preferential option" for them. In the breaking and eating of the bread, this preferential option was allegorized and became visible. Thus, the gesture of offering the bread symbolizes the commitment and surrender of Jesus for us and for our world.

Suggestions for Workshop 2:

What does the breaking of the bread indicate?

1. *Please read* Mark 2:13–17; 6:30–44; 8:1–9; Luke 19:1–10 or alternatively act these scenes out.

2. *Please discuss* first: What is the common background of all of these scenes? What sort of people meet with Jesus?

3. *Please read* now Mark 14:22–25.

4. *Please discuss* then: To what extent do these Bible texts shed new light on the words of institution spoken during the Last Supper?

Eating Establishes Human Community

Eucharist gives peace, strength, [and] inspiration. Eucharist makes grace something to eat and savor (if the wine is good!).

—*Val From*

Communion is the company of Jesus and of fellow Christians, perceived in an emotive fashion. In the bread and wine (and tasting and seeing) we again draw near to the company and presence of Jesus in our consciousness, and we draw closer to each other through him.

—*Christel Paladey* (46 years old)

Unfortunately, many people today have lost the sense that common meals have the power to establish human community. This was different in antiquity. In ancient Greece, a house community ate together; a foreigner could not just randomly participate. Aristotle called the members of a house community *homokapoi*, which means "those who eat at the same table." If a foreigner was invited, this person was first led to the hearth, the center of the house, and was asked to participate in a meal. This meant the foreigner was more or less incorporated into the family; this procedure was the precondition for further contact with family members. Meals were an indicator of who belonged to a social group and who did not.

For this reason, ancient Greeks and Romans frequently held *symposia* (this term is the plural of *symposium* and refers to lavish convivial banquets). It was important to participate in *symposia* in order to establish and preserve social contacts. The social standing and reputation of a person or family broadly depended on who invited them to a *symposium*. Similar practices still exist today in many cultures and societies. Therefore, social anthropologists call such shared meals "incorporation rituals."

In ancient times it was, furthermore, common knowledge that bread, once broken and shared among many people lead to inextricable unity. For instance, during a wedding ceremony in Ancient Rome, a bride and a groom ate bread together. The power to forge common bonds amongst those who eat bread is alluded to in the word "companion." It stems from the French *compagnon*, which is in turn derived from the Latin word *companio*. Both words contain the word "bread," namely *panis* in Latin and *pain* in French. This means that a companion is defined as somebody with (Latin: *cum*) whom one eats bread.

Ancient Israel and Judah had a similar understanding.

Different festivals were celebrated throughout their traditional yearly cycle (Exod. 23:14–19; Lev. 23; Num. 28–29; also see above, pp. 64–65). Most of these festivals involved celebrations with much eating and drinking, and during this revelry, one reaffirmed one's own identity and established or maintained social contacts with others. This is similar to the practice still carried on by many Native American tribes in North America. They gather in annual "pow-wows" (or "powwows") where drumming, dancing, and eating take place—often making important political decisions and tending to cultural affairs. In modern Western cultures, family reunions on occasions such as Christmas, Easter, Thanksgiving, or to celebrate baptisms, weddings, and funerals typically feature large communal meals. They are family gatherings that define who belongs to the family and who does not.

At the time of Jesus, people were well aware of the community-forging power of meals. With the above-mentioned understanding of the significance of shared meals in ancient times, it is almost self-explanatory that Jesus was sharply criticized for eating together with tax collectors and sinners (Mark 2:16). Underlying such criticism was the concern that this kind of conduct would establish a lasting association with social outsiders or contemporaries not befitting one's rank. But for Jesus, it was these non-traditional associations that were a sign and expression of God's Kingdom on earth. In one of his letters to the Christian community in Corinth, Paul later speaks of this particular aspect of the Last Supper:

> The cup of the blessing that we bless, is it not the communion of the blood of Christ? The bread that we break, is it not the communion of the body of Christ? Because there is one bread, we who are many are one body as we all partake of the one bread. (1 Cor. 10:16–17)

Drinking and eating bind people together. Accordingly, Paul refers to the bread at Communion as the "body of Christ," but he also uses the same term of the people partaking of that bread (1 Cor. 12:12–31). Human contact and integration were distinctive signs of Christ's mission. Whoever partakes of Communion recalls Jesus and his life and remembers that Jesus died because he did not always conform to the expectations of others.

Unfortunately, our own modern fast food culture has lost sight of most of these social dimensions of eating. Yet a few examples of the unifying power of dining in common do exist. In July 2009, the President of the United States, Barack Obama, attempted to settle a dispute between Henry Louis Gates, a professor at Harvard University, and James M. Crowley, a policeman from Cambridge, Massachusetts—and the President used an invitation to a joint dinner to accomplish this. The dispute arose because Crowley had mistakenly arrested Gates (who is African-American) for allegedly trying to break in a house that was his own home. This case caused controversy in the U.S. because of possible racist motives for the arrest. At first, even President Obama criticized Crowley's actions. In order to resolve the tension, the President decided to invite Gates and Crowley to a shared meal in the White House. President Obama's gesture achieved its reconciliatory effect.

It may also be noted that eating makes possible contact and the establishment of relations in an elementary manner and way, even when other forms of communication are not possible. We experience this time and again when a child is born. How can we communicate with the baby? Obviously many months go by before we can speak together. Until then, the parents' care and love find other forms of expression—above all else by providing proper food for its nourishment. It is apparent to whom the baby belongs and who the care-givers are, because mostly the baby will be nourished by parents, relatives, or by people especially called for this task. On account of dietary practices, social relations can be recognized—those who eat together belong together!

Moreover, eating is the most basic form of communicating in this world—even working between different species. This is apparent when we observe the feeding of animals. Aside of course from specially trained house pets, there is no real conversation possible with the likes of birds, dogs, cats, or fish. Most animals flee outright when they see that humans approach them. Yet we all have experienced that when we bring along food, wild animals may come up to us under certain circumstances. Thus, it is possible to have "close encounters" with another species, even with the ducks on the lake in city parks, the fish in a fish tank, or goats in the petting zoo.

Existence on this earth is characterized by great distinctions between various creatures, and specifically humans define themselves from one another on the grounds of nationality, descent, language, social class, religion, political beliefs, gender, age, and so forth. Conflicts and even wars are frequently sparked because of such differences. In view of this, common meals and the celebration of festivals are possibilities for the overcoming of such differences. Likewise, the Last Supper was an institution established by Jesus for just such a purpose. It was and is an institution that expresses God's love for all humans. Luke, for example, mentions how the first Christians met in their private homes where they "broke bread . . . and ate their food with joy" (Acts 2:46). It is no surprise that sharing the gospel, which means the good news of God's love, had such an effect on the first Christians.

Without you
who wandered many roads and
left crucial footprints in the sand
we can't go on at all

Without you
and your radiant gaze full of light
which opened the eyes of the blind
our candles shine no longer bright

Without you
and the irresistible tone
of your voice that teaches us to share
we'd still run out of bread at home

Without you
the generous guest
at the wedding at Cana
our wine will not last for the never-ending feast

—Lothar Zenetti

Whoever participates in Communion belongs to the body of Christ and is a child of God. In Communion, God's grace becomes visible and can be perceived in an emotive fashion. We are reminded that God's grace and love for humanity are not perceived only through the intellect by hearing teaching or preaching. Whoever participates in Communion experiences God's grace and love with the senses through touch and taste. Participants also experience God's grace and love as a social phenomenon because of the integrative power of communion that allows people to experience God's grace and love in a way they might not be able to articulate. These experiences are part of following Christ.

If Communion is the center of Christian devotion and theology, Christians won't behave toward others (particularly non-Christians) in such a way as to indoctrinate them. Those who do so most often only attempt to expound their own sense of superiority. Yet when Christian communities are shaped by the practice of Communion, they will gladly welcome others to the celebration. Such celebrations belong to the sphere of experience, of sharing, and of common joy.

Conclusion: How does eating establish human community? In Greco-Roman antiquity, *symposia* (lavish banquets) were occasions for initiating and maintaining social contacts. This was also true for the various yearly festivals observed in the early Jewish tradition. Moreover, eating together allows connections to be formed when other forms of communication are not possible. In the Last Supper, Jesus has established a ritualized meal against the perennial tendency of humans to exclude others for whatever reasons they can think of. Communion thereby signifies that the Kingdom of God is fundamentally open to all people.

Suggestions for Workshop 3:

Eating as the basis for human society

Watch the movie *Babette's Feast* (the original Danish release is called *Babettes Gaestebud*) by Gabriel Axel, which won an Academy Award in 1987. Or read the novel by author Karen Blixen on which the film was based. The theme of the film and book is that a meal prepared with love—and also a considerable expenditure of money and effort—is able to accomplish great things. It can help a group of people to regain unity and happiness, not the least pious folk who had been divided from each other by mutual grudges and ill-will.

1. *Please discuss*: Have you ever experienced how a meal can establish or reestablish unity amongst people?

2. *Please discuss*: In your social environment or in your church, are there people who are at odds with

each other? Or are there quarrels between you and somebody else? What could be done to encounter each other anew and regain unity?

Summary: The Early Christian Communion

God's assurance of forgiveness is received with the bread and wine and the words of promise.

—*Pastor David Hunter (Lutheran)*

In the Bible and in Christian churches, there is no uniform or univocal understanding or explanation of the celebration with bread and wine. After all, there is not even a universally acknowledged term for it. Nevertheless, several biblical aspects can be gathered that each allow us to articulate different meanings of Communion. These have been described in the previous sections of this book.

In doing so, it became clear that Communion is to be understood in one sense as a ritualized meal. Since all people regularly eat meals, the symbolism of Communion is fundamentally accessible to everyone. Eating especially provides a basic form of contact as a remedy against social exclusion of every kind.

It also became clear on the foregoing pages that Communion refers to the religious traditions of the Old Testament and early Judaism. Thus, the drinking from the cup relates to concepts of atonement. The words "this is my blood of the covenant" refer specifically to a central text from the Torah that describes the covenant sealed between God and Israel at Mt. Sinai. During this covenant, sins are forgiven through the sprinkling of blood of sacrificial animals; the Israelites are then consecrated and made holy. Because of this explicit reference, the drinking of the wine that represents the blood of Jesus is to be understood in an analogous way. Whoever drinks from the cup is consecrated and belongs to the people of God. According to traditional Jewish conceptions, a new covenant is sealed between God and humanity through Communion.

In addition, the Last Supper, which Jesus celebrated with his disciples, was a Passover meal and thus a part of the Jewish tradition at the time of Jesus. Passover institutionalized the remembrance of the salvation of the Israelites from slavery. This understanding informs the eating of the bread that facilitates remembrance of Jesus, who dedicated his life to the needy and the socially outcast. This dimension of his mission was always apparent in the various meals he shared with people considered "sinners." By such inclinations, Jesus fundamentally questioned certain religious and social conventions. The results were conflicts with the religious and political authorities. Jesus did not avoid these conflicts, which in the end led to his death on the cross. The blessing, breaking, sharing, and eating of the bread that is his body all signify visibly that he cared for, and gave his life for all people, particularly for the disadvantaged. To that extent, Jesus is present in the Christian celebration of Communion. These considerations make clear that the cup and the "blood of the new covenant" refer primarily to Old Testament conceptions of atonement, whereas the breaking of the bread refers to the courageous and loving mission of Jesus for others that is the central theme of the New Testament in general and the Gospels in particular.

Chapter 4

COMMUNION IN MODERN CHURCH PRACTICE

The Eucharist is a hole in the universe connecting us to God and all creation, transcending sin, pain, separation, and our fallen nature, [and] returning us to wholeness.

—Paul Blaser

Recently while on vacation, I personally witnessed a substitute pastor from Bavaria invite all people of whatever denomination or age to receive Communion. Prior to that, people who didn't feel comfortable participating in Communion would often leave the church in time; that was also the case here to some extent.

—Anonymous

In this concluding chapter, I shall try to connect insights about Communion from the previous chapters to modern worship practices of various denominations and churches. Each tradition shares understandings and essential aspects of the Last Supper that we have covered at length in this book. The question to ponder now is: In what way and to what extent does our worship practice correspond to its biblical foundations? The following observations are in no way comprehensive; they are only meant to provide some initial suggestions for reflecting on, and perhaps adjusting several basic aspects of our modern worship practices.

1. *The Last Supper and biblical proclamation*: In the previous chapters, I pointed out first of all that the breaking of the bread is connected to the life story of Jesus. Accordingly, the cup of the "new covenant" takes up priestly conceptions of atonement as described in the Old Testament. It is fundamental to recognize that both bread and wine have at all times referred back to biblical traditions. In most celebrations of Communion, it is customary to include readings (and homilies) from these Bible passages. This custom ensures that the symbolism and meaning of the Last Supper becomes or remains understandable to modern people. This provision also guarantees that the eating of the bread and drinking from the cup is a "remembrance" of Jesus (1 Cor. 11:24–25). Thus, not every possible celebration with bread and wine necessarily has the characteristics of Communion, which is the combination of scriptural reading, Christian proclamation, and the rite of distributing and consuming bread and wine.

2. *Communion and biblical texts*: In our church celebrations of Communion, extensive passages from the New Testament are often recited. Biblical texts are of course integrated into other sections of worship as well, for example when the "Our Father" is prayed (adopted from Matt. 6:9–13). Yet some denominations have the habit to include extensive readings from biblical passages at that occasion. It's also typical that, beyond the recitation of words, the actions described in the text are enacted, in so far as bread and wine are distributed and consumed by the congregation. Aspects like these make the celebration of Communion the apex and central aspect of worship.

It is also worth mentioning that our churches, with such enactments, follow an explicit prompt: "*Do this* in remembrance of me." Jesus said these words to his disciples during the Last Supper when giving them bread and the cup of wine (1 Cor. 11:24–25). It is appropriate, therefore, during worship today to *do* the same and offer both bread and wine to the congregation.

3. *Communion and the Community of God*: In the biblical texts which constitute the foundation of the Christian celebration of Communion, we find the words of institution said over the bread and wine: "This is my body (that is for you)" and "this cup is the new covenant in my blood (which is poured out for many)" (see Table 1 on pp. 35–37). With these words, Jesus gave guidelines for how he understood the original Last Supper and how he wanted others to understand it. Their implications

should be appreciated for the worship praxis of contemporary Christians.

Here I would like to refer to one detail that only appears to be incidental: the bread is "given for you" and the wine is "poured out for many." In the original Greek passages, the "you" is plural; there is no singular "you" that would refer to an individual. As for the wine, it is definitely said that it is "poured out for many" and not just "only for you." The same is true for comparable statements on the subject of salvation in the New Testament. For example, in Paul's letter to the Romans, salvation is described as applying to the whole community: "What then are we to say about these things? If God is *for us*, who is *against us*?" (Rom. 8:31). Other comparable statements in the New Testament are likewise in the plural (e.g., Rom. 5:6–9; 1 Cor. 15:3; 2 Cor. 5:14–15; Eph. 5:1–2).

In our modern churches, the words of institution, "the body of Christ, given for *you*—the blood of Christ, shed for *you*," should not be heard as invitations to individuals. Communion is always associated with an invitation to gather in a community. In fact, salvation is made real and tangible in communities of people who encounter each other to read the biblical texts together in order to understand them and meet God, and who celebrate, eat, and drink in common. "Come and see that the Lord is good." The Christian church is not so much about individual as about collective redemption.

4. *Different forms of celebrating Communion*: Today, Communion is celebrated in a variety of forms. In some churches, worshippers line up to approach

the altar and receive bread and wine. In other churches, participants kneel in the area before the altar. Yet in both cases, it is typical that participants are permitted to approach the place of greater holiness—the place where the minister or priest stands and leads the worship service.

Participants at Communion are allowed to approach this privileged and sacred area around the communion table or altar as far as possible. This prerogative can be explained through the drinking from the cup that contains the "blood of the new covenant" and brings about atonement. As such, the drinking of the cup affects forgiveness of sins (Matt. 26:28) and sanctifies the worshippers (see above, pp. 71–74). The approach of the especially holy space around the altar is in a certain sense similar to the situation at Mt. Sinai, where the Israelites were allowed to climb up that holy mountain and then shared a meal in the presence of God (see above, pp. 62–64, 68).

According to an alternative worship practice, the participants of Communion do not approach the communion table or altar at all, but remain seated where they are. Bread and wine are then distributed throughout the pews from one member of the congregation to the next, with the words of institution (or a Bible passage) being recited over them. This form may be explained by the understanding that the individual participants are consecrated by the effective forgiveness of sins. They are then made similar to the priests who, in worship at the Jewish temple, were also consecrated through a blood rite and were ordained by it (Exod. 29:19–21; Lev. 8:23–24; also see above, pp. 67–73).

HISTORY AND BACKGROUND:

Sacred Space and Holiness

Buildings or spaces in which people gather to worship God and pray are considered holy. They are accordingly called "sacred spaces" from the Latin word *sacrum*, which means "holy" or "set apart." In these buildings, however, not every area is considered equally holy or sacred. To state the matter simply, the area in which worshippers enter into the church and then stay throughout the worship service is considered relatively less holy. The space in which the minister or priest leads the service is correspondingly associated with a higher degree of sacredness. So it is that this space contains sacred objects, for example the altar, Bibles, and large crosses or crucifixes. In Catholic churches, the tabernacle, in particular, is placed here. It contains the hosts that, according to Catholic belief, are the body of Christ.

Usually the altar is elevated and steps are present which lead up to the area immediately around it. Frequently, it is also laid out with special carpets (often red in color), and it is set apart by the erection of banisters, handrails, or the like. All this serves to set apart the area around the altar as a place of greater holiness; and it signals that the "ordinary" worshippers do not have free and random access to it.

Due to this consecration, the participants are able to take on and fulfill a sort of "priestly" office. After the individual participants have received bread and wine, they take an active part in its further distribution.

5. *Communion and Atonement*: Of course, as I have stated above, ideas such as sacrifice and atonement are often misunderstood and rejected nowadays. Thus, it is advisable to study the underlying biblical texts and to explain the concepts to Christian worshippers. It is also possible that occasionally such explanations may be used during the actual celebration of Communion itself. Thus the minister of the Protestant-Lutheran All-Saints Community in Kelowna, Canada, used labels such as "presence" and "life" in the place of the words "bread" and "blood."[25] New participants, who were not very familiar with the specialized terminologies of the Bible or the church, welcomed these changes. Of course, we must consider that such clarifying terminology can never cover every shade of meaning inherent in the underlying symbolic terminology. What is more, there is also the danger that, under certain circumstances, misunderstandings could become institutionalized due to alternative labels, or that the traditions embedded in the biblical texts may get lost. The latter, however, also occurs when antiquated terminology is simply used in modern churches without any attempt of exploring and explaining its meaning.

6. *Communion and Social Companionship*: Particularly in churches of North America, it is customary after Sunday worship services to have "fellowship time," where coffee, juice, and cookies are made available. The purpose is to motivate the worshippers to stay a bit longer and socialize. Occasionally, lunch is served as well. These practices are similar to the customs of the early church, since Christians back

then celebrated Communion as a special part of a larger meal (see above, pp. 18 and 29). In this way, there is more time for the worshippers to become acquainted with one another, and poorer members are able to eat their fill alongside everyone else.

7. *Fasting for Communion*? For this reason one may find grounds for questioning a practice that is still observed sometimes today. In some churches and denominations, worshippers are instructed to observe a fast before appearing for Communion. Whatever the reasons for such an appeal, it is clear that no biblical passage on the Last Supper has any such requirement. Furthermore, it contradicts the Last Supper of Jesus and the custom of the early Christian church. In both cases, the actual celebration happened in the context of a larger meal, so that no one could have logically been fasting before it.

8. *Frequency of Celebration of Communion*: For many Christians, Communion is the climax of worship and a sacrament, yet not all denominations celebrate it with equal frequency. This is perhaps in part due to the New Testament texts that feature no information on how often Communion should be celebrated. One note in Acts 2:42 nevertheless mentions the "breaking of bread" alongside the teaching of the apostles, mutual fellowship, and prayers, suggesting that Communion was a characteristic and regular activity of the early Christian congregation. Today, Communion is celebrated every day in some denominations; elsewhere it is a regular part of Sunday services.

Other denominations celebrate it less often, even as little as four times a year. In fact, the Jehovah's Witnesses view Communion primarily as a continuation of the traditional Passover feast, and so they celebrate it only once a year (see above, p. 10). Here again it is apparent that different Christian churches and denominations have never been in exact agreement as to the meaning of Communion. The conflicting interpretations determine, among other things, the frequency and timing of its celebration.

9. *Participation in Communion*: Who should take part in Communion? According to the Gospels, Jesus often accepted the dinner invitations of sinners and other social outcasts. Generally speaking, he concerned himself with very diverse sets of people. His followers were accordingly a diverse and colorful lot, and an exoteric one open to all (see above, p. 98). In this way, it was made apparent that God's love is boundless and extended to all people. At the original Last Supper, Jesus did not even turn away Judas, even though he knew that this disciple was about to betray him. The Gospels present the Last Supper, therefore, as an "open house" or "no jacket required" affair, not a "special invitation only" one. Fundamentally, Communion is no institution of exclusion.

I myself was once excluded from Communion. In a church in Boston, Massachusetts, the Communion proper began after the worship service had been going on for about three hours. I joined those waiting in a long line to take part in Communion. Just as I was about to receive the bread, to my astonishment, I was asked by the priest whether I belonged to his particular denomination. I quietly replied, "I am Christian" (no pun intended). The priest repeated his question, and this time I answered, "I am a Protestant Christian." At that point, he told me to return to my seat. I was not allowed to receive Communion in his church. I don't want to reflect here upon my immediate thoughts and feelings; nevertheless, it does seem to me an abuse of Communion to exclude Christians from participating who had permission to join in the preceding worship service. These ideas also apply in principle to the practice of certain churches and denominations to exclude some members due to specific internal criteria. Communion should fundamentally be open for all who are baptized— and should not be a means of broadcasting the exclusion of people.

10. *Communion and Mission*: It often becomes apparent that the way in which such aspects about Communion have been dealt with in praxis is more than just a theological word game. Such questions do have practical repercussions. Among other consequences, the answers to these questions determine how churches relate to non-members or non-Christians. In regard to missionary activity, for instance, such rules for observance of Communion do in the final analysis have important effects. The way we observe Communion determines how our churches are perceived by outsiders. It determines whether others ever get a sense that our churches take forgiveness of sins seriously. It determines whether others feel how God's love is

real among people. It determines whether others have the privilege to experience that our churches celebrate Communion according to the gospel of Jesus Christ. It determines whether others will ever experience what a difference a meal makes for the world.

ADDITIONAL INFORMATION

Further Recommended Readings

The following is a list of recommended literature (in alphabetical order) for those interested in further information on the topic of this book:

Accola, Louis W. *Given for You: Reflections on the Meaning of the Lord's Supper*. Minneapolis: Augsburg Fortress, 2007.

> Accola describes the Lord's Supper as a meal to which all Christians are invited to experience unity among each other and the presence of Jesus Christ. The Lord's Supper is God's renewed covenant. Humans can never earn being part of this covenant, yet God invites sinners.

Davies, Horton. *Bread of Life and Cup of Joy: Newer Ecumenical Perspectives on the Eucharist*. Eugene, OR: Wipf and Stock, 1999.

> Davies shows, among other things, how the Eucharist has the power of shaping the spirituality of the church. To that end, he provides many examples of liturgical texts and prayers that show how a Eucharistic celebration may be

done. Moreover, Davies includes a notable chapter on "The Eucharist as Liberation and Social Justice" (pp. 180–219).

Davis, Thomas J. *This is my Body: The Presence of Christ in Reformation Thought.* Grand Rapids, MI: Baker Academic, 2008.

Davis presents a fair overview of how some of the leaders of the Protestant Reformation, among them Martin Luther and John Calvin, have interpreted the Last Supper. The book is written for an academic audience.

Donnelly, Doris, ed. *Sacraments and Justice.* Collegeville, MN: Liturgical Press, 2014.

This volume explains the connection between the seven sacraments recognized by the Roman Catholic Church and justice. It therefore features an essay by Michael S. Driscoll on "Eucharist and Justice" (pp. 32–44). It starts with a moving eyewitness account of a Eucharist celebrated on an altar, half of which is on the U.S. side of the border and half is on the Mexico side, despite a chain link fence marking the border. The mass is dedicated to the commemoration of those who have died while crossing this border. Driscoll's essay repeatedly reminds readers that those who participate in the Eucharist are called into the one body of Jesus Christ.

Erlander, Daniel. *A Place for You: My Holy Communion Book.* Freeland, WA: self-published, 1999.

A richly illustrated book for children about Communion; it is also fit for church classes on that same topic. Erlander interprets Communion as an indication that God loves all people and certainly has a place for everybody.

Fulkerson, Mary McClintock and Shoop, Marcia W. Mount. *A Body Broken, A Body Betrayed: Race, Memory, and Eucharist in White-Dominant Churches*. Eugene, OR: Cascade Books, 2015.

> This book looks particularly at the issue of race and privilege in the context of the celebration of Eucharist. It invites members of predominantly white Protestant churches in the United States of America to engage in a process of self-examination and recognize the sacrament as a means of effective racial integration.

Lange, Dirk G. *Trauma Recalled: Liturgy, Disruption, and Theology*. Minneapolis: Fortress Press, 2009.

> According to Lange, Christianity was born out of the traumatic event of the death of Jesus on the cross. Also, the celebration of the Eucharist goes back to this trauma; it was a means of overcoming it for both the disciples of Jesus and later Christian communities. Great reformers like Martin Luther saw it as a liturgical manifestation of God's grace. Lange, who is writing for an academic audience, also comments (pp. 143–53) on the Eucharistic instructions in chapters 9–10 of the *Didache*, the *Teaching of the Twelve Apostles*, which might date to approximately 50 CE.

Pitre, Brant. *Jesus and the Jewish Roots of the Eucharist: Unlocking the Secrets of the Last Supper*. New York: Doubleday, 2011.

> As the title indicates, Pitre's book is an attempt to understand the Eucharist in the framework of Judaism at the time of Jesus. It is thus similar to some of the perspective of the present book. On pages 50–76, the author discusses the implications of the Jewish Passover celebration for the Eucharist.

Porter, Thomas W., ed. *Conflict and Communion: Reconciliation and Restorative Justice at Christ's Table.* Nashville: Upper Room Books, 2006.

This volume's editor, a lawyer, mediator, and minister, gathered individual articles by contributors from diverse denominations. They all link communion and conflict resolution and therefore show the usefulness of religion for "real" issues.

Skinner, Douglas B. *At the Lord's Table: Communion Prayers for All Seasons.* St. Louis: Chalice Press, 2006.

This book contains a compilation of prayers that are set in relation to texts from the Bible. They are also arranged according to liturgical seasons of the church.

Smith, Gordon T. *A Holy Meal: The Lord's Supper in the Life of the Church.* Grand Rapids, MI: Baker Academic, 2005.

Gordon T. Smith connects the interpretation of biblical texts with church traditions and practices. One of many points of his argument is that the church does not celebrate a "renewed" sacrifice of Jesus on the cross during Communion, but remembers him as the resurrected one and becomes part of his body (pp. 61–65).

Smith, Dennis E. *From Symposium to Eucharist: The Banquet in the Early Christian World.* Minneapolis: Fortress Press, 2003.

Dennis E. Smith presents an academic study of the role, custom, and practice of banquets in antiquity. He suggests that such celebrations were usually scenarios where a community of equals was being constituted despite their differences in status. They were also occasions of collective joy. Therefore, early Christians habitually had meals when they met in groups.

In addition to these books, Bible dictionaries and lexicons are helpful resources for further studies of biblical themes. For example, in the *Dictionary of the Bible and Western Culture*, edited by Mary Ann Beavis and Michael J. Gilmour (Sheffield: Sheffield Phoenix Press, 2011), the following articles are relevant to the topic of this book:

"Atonement" by Christian A. Eberhart
"Bread" by Christopher Francis
"Eucharist" by Andrew J. Waskey
"Lord's Supper" by Christian A. Eberhart
"Passover" by Daniel Maoz
"Sacrifice" by Christian A. Eberhart
"Wine" by Kyle D. Potter

Summary of Suggestions for Workshops

Suggestions for Workshop 1:

What does the "blood of the new covenant" mean?

1. *Please read* Exodus 24:1–11; Exodus 29:19–21; Leviticus 14:10–20. You can also act out these scenes by having different groups play one of these Bible texts.

2. *Please discuss* first: What ritual elements do these biblical texts have in common? What do the texts say about effects of the rituals?

3. *Please discuss* then: Do these Bible texts help you to gain a better understanding of the account of the Last Supper in Mark 14:22–25 or of the celebration of Communion in your church?

Suggestions for Workshop 2:

What does the breaking of the bread indicate?

1. *Please read* Mark 2:13–17; 6:30–44; 8:1–9; Luke 19:1–10 or alternatively act these scenes out.

2. *Please discuss* first: What is the common background of all of these scenes? What sort of people meet with Jesus?

3. *Please read* now Mark 14:22–25.

4. *Please discuss then*: To what extent do these Bible texts shed new light on the words of institution spoken during the Last Supper?

Suggestions for Workshop 3: Eating as the basis for human society

Watch the movie *Babette's Feast* (the original Danish release is called *Babettes Gaestebud*) by Gabriel Axel, which won an Academy Award in 1987. Or read the novel by author Karen Blixen on which the film was based. The theme of the film and book is that a meal prepared with love—and also a considerable expenditure of money and effort—is able to accomplish great things. It can help a group of people to regain unity and happiness, not the least pious folk who had been divided from each other by mutual grudges and ill-will.

1. *Please discuss*: Have you ever experienced how a meal can establish or reestablish unity amongst people?

2. *Please discuss*: In your social environment or in your church, are there people who are at odds with each other? Or are there quarrels between you and somebody else? What could be done to encounter each other anew and regain unity?

The Location of the Last Supper of Jesus: The "Upper Room"

According to Mark 14:14–15, Jesus and his disciples ate the Last Supper in a guest room described as "a large upper room, spread [with couches], and ready." It is therefore known simply as the "Upper Room." This room was located in Jerusalem on Mount Zion. The following images show a room at that location, which is identified today as the "Upper Room." (Photos taken by C. A. Eberhart)

The "Upper Room" is located on the left side of this courtyard on Mount Zion, Jerusalem.

The door to the "Upper Room."

The window in the "Upper Room."

The interior of the "Upper Room."

The construction date of the present-day building is difficult to determine. The columns and pillars and the Gothic-style vaulted ceiling of the room, considered in light of certain historical aspects, make a date between the 12th and 13th century CE plausible. Hence, the original room from the time of Jesus could have been renovated or reconstructed later on.

Credits: Poetry by
Lothar Zenetti

Poesie
Was Jesus für mich ist?
Die wunderbare Zeitvermehrung
In: Lothar Zenetti, *Auf Seiner Spur: Texte gläubiger Zuversicht*,
    Mainz: Matthias Grünewald, 2002.

Lied zur Eucharistie
Ohne Dich
In: Lothar Zenetti, *Sieben Farben hat das Licht: Texte, die den
    Tag begleiten*, Munich: Pfeiffer, 1987.

English translations:
by Véronique A. and Christian A. Eberhart.

Endnotes

1. See my following books: Eberhart, Christian A. *The Sacrifice of Jesus: Understanding Atonement Biblically* (Facets), Minneapolis: Fortress Press, 2011; Eberhart, Christian A. *Kultmetaphorik und Christologie: Opfer- und Sühneterminologie im Neuen Testament* (Wissenschaftliche Untersuchungen zum Neuen Testament 306), Tübingen: Mohr Siebeck, 2013.

2. The oldest manuscripts of the Gospel according to Mark end with the report of the empty tomb (Mark 16:1–8). The so-called longer ending of Mark (16:9–20) concerning the appearances and heavenly ascension of the resurrected Jesus (respectively another, even shorter text) was added only later to the Gospel.

3. In following chapters, we will explore the significance of the Passover in more detail.

4. Biblical passages cited in this book have been translated by me from the Hebrew or Greek original texts of the Old and New Testament, respectively. My translations are guided by the attempt to achieve a close and precise rendition of these texts, even though this may imply that, at times, the "elegance" of expression is somewhat compromised. I have occasionally added words in parentheses, which generally help the understanding of the phrase.

5. The Book of Genesis is also called "The First Book of Moses," and the Book of Deuteronomy is also called "The Fifth Book of Moses."

6. See Chapter 3, starting on p. 45.

7. Older Bible translations often render this phrase, "And when they were sitting at table" which does not correspond with ancient meal customs. Greco-Roman antiquity did not know of dining tables with chairs to sit on. Instead, communal meals were usually shared in a formal dining room. Such a room was usually called *triclinium* in Greek, conveying that there were three couches (*klinai*) with surfaces sloped at approximately 10 degrees. Participants in the meal would recline on pillows on these couches in a semi-recumbent position. The couches were arranged in a u-shape around a table on which the food would be presented; the fourth side was left open to allow service to the table.

8. Qumran was the site of an ancient Jewish community until 68 CE, when Roman soldiers captured it. Probably due to disagreements with the religious establishment in Jerusalem, this community had withdrawn to a location in the desert and close to the Dead Sea. The people of this community stored many scrolls in eleven caves in an around Qumran; the scrolls were found and published starting in 1947.

9. For the concepts of "sin" and "sinners" in the Bible, see below (pp. 61–62).

10. See chapter 3, starting on p. 45.

11. See below, p. 98 and p. 110.

12. The book called "The Teaching of the Twelve Apostles" (*Didache*) was probably composed between the year 100 and

180 CE. It had, for a long time, canonical status, which means it was part of the New Testament.

13. In the Roman Catholic Church the term "sacrifice" is used in conjunction with that of "Mass." This makes explicit reference to the idea that, according to Roman Catholic teachings, the bread and wine are really transformed into the flesh and blood of Jesus at the moment when the priest pronounces the words of institution.

14. According to the texts of the New Testament that tell of the Last Supper, the meal of Jesus was probably not the main Passover meal. It is possible that Jesus and his disciples celebrated a less formal Passover meal during the week of preparations before the actual festival. The Passover feast proper would see, in accordance with the prescriptions of the Old Testament, the use of only unleavened bread (Exod. 12:8, 39). The bread which Jesus distributed to his disciples at the Last Supper was, however, made with yeast, as the Greek word *artos* in Mark 14:22 suggests. This type of bread was strictly forbidden during the actual Passover. In addition to these observations, the enemies of Jesus planned to have him killed before the Passover feast (Mark 14:1–2). Finally, the crucifixion itself occurred on "the day of Preparation"—that is, the day before the Passover feast (Mark 15:42).

15. The book of Exodus is also known as "The Second Book of Moses."

16. The book of Leviticus is also called "The Third Book of Moses."

17. This is different in many countries of Africa and Asia, where sacrificial rituals are still being practiced today. There are, for example, various sacrificial rituals in brahmanical Hinduism;

these have repeatedly been compared with those of the Old Testament or Judaism.

18. It is difficult to say when exactly this text was composed. Nowadays the three Johannine letters are generally held to have been composed before the year 100 CE. Suggestions for a date range between the years 60 and 100. In comparison, scholars have, until recently, considered the book Fourth Maccabees as older than the Johannine letters. According to recent suggestions, however, this book was rather composed toward the end of the 1st century or at the beginning of the 2nd century CE. By the way, all Four Books of the Maccabees, including this one, belonged to the Greek translation of the Hebrew Bible; thus it belonged to the Old Testament version of early Christianity.

19. As a matter of fact, the Old Testament term of "sacrifice" is, properly speaking, not restricted to animal sacrifices or to sacrificial rituals. In Numbers 7, even covered wagons, together with the oxen that pulled them (7:3), as well as silver plates (7:13), a gold dish (7:14) and various animals (7:15–17) are called "sacrifice" (likewise in 7:19–83). This more encompassing use of the term "sacrifice" is, however, obscured in modern English Bible translations. Numbers 7 constantly employs the Hebrew word *Qorban*, which is the most common priestly term for "sacrifice," yet most English translations of Numbers 7 simply render it as "gift."

20. The Old Testament story of the Prophet Elisha has the most in common with the narratives of the multiplication of the bread in Mark 6:30–44 and Mark 8:1–9. In Second Kings 4:42–44, Elisha instructs a man to distribute twenty loaves of barley bread to a hundred people, and after they all ate there were still leftovers. References to this are still found in Judaism today, as for example in the 18th century CE Hasidic history of

Endnotes

Rabbi Elimelech of Lizhensk. Moreover there are also certain similarities with the feeding of the Israelites in the wilderness with Manna (Exod. 16), which in turn is referenced later in the Second Apocalypse of Baruch 29:8.

21. In accordance with ancient views, the word "heart" indicates here the faculty of intellectual understanding (for further clarification see above, p. 74).

22. Moreover, the history of early Christianity was at first marked persistently by the celebration of meals. Christianity was indeed an extremely diverse and geographically dispersed movement. Nevertheless, until the 3rd or 4th century CE, Christians met with each other primarily in the context of common meals and understood themselves as "meal-societies" (according to Matthias Klinghardt, *Gemeinschaftsmahl und Mahlgemeinschaft: Soziologie und Liturgie frühchristlicher Mahlfeiern*, Tübingen, Basel: A. Francke Verlag, 1996).

23. It should be noted that, for the past centuries, the theme of the real presence has been explained in different ways. The Roman Catholic Church and some Eastern Churches are of the opinion that Jesus is "really present" because during the celebration of the Eucharist, the bread and wine are really transformed into the flesh and blood of Jesus, even though their outward appearances ("accidents") that are visible to humans remain unaltered. This process is called "transubstantiation," and it is said to occur when the priest pronounces the words of institution. The Reformation rejected this idea. Martin Luther nevertheless maintained the real presence according to his work *Vom Abendmahl Christi: Bekenntnis* published in 1528 (*On the Last Supper of Christ: Confession*). In doing so he distinguished between three different modes of Christ's existence—a bodily one, an imperceptible spiritual one, and a heavenly one. Thus, Luther could describe Christ as the principle of creation, among

other things, and posit that Christ is present in all expressions of the created world, including bread and wine.

24. Michael Welker, *Was geht vor beim Abendmahl?* 3rd ed. Gütersloh: Gütersloher Verlagshaus, 2005, p. 97: "Es ist die schöpferische, anderen zugute kommende Hingabe, das schöpferische freie Sich-selbst-Hineinversetzen in andere, die in dieser Identifikation mit dem Brot und dem Wein Ausdruck findet. In dem in der Mahlfeier in Erinnerung an Christi Hingabe ausgeteilten Brot wird das Wesentliche, das Entscheidende, die Wahrheit der Person Christi konzentriert vergegenwärtigt."

25. From a news report appearing in the church journal *Canada Lutheran* 23/8, p. 17.

Index of Biblical Passages

Index of Biblical Passages

www.ingramcontent.com/pod-product-compliance
Lightning Source LLC
Chambersburg PA
CBHW071445090426
42737CB00011B/1781